CRYSTAL LAND

CRYSTAL
LAND

Artifice
in Nabokov's
English Novels

JULIA BADER

UNIVERSITY OF
CALIFORNIA PRESS

BERKELEY, LOS ANGELES, LONDON

University of California Press
Berkeley and Los Angeles, California
University of California Press, Ltd.
London, England
Copyright © 1972, by
The Regents of the University of California
ISBN: 0-520-02167-3
Library of Congress Catalog Card Number: 72-182277
Printed in the United States of America

To
MARK SCHORER
with respect and affection

CONTENTS

ACKNOWLEDGMENTS

Many people have assisted me generously: Emily Izsak and Allan Brick with early encouragement and example, Robert Alter with numerous suggestions, Norman S. Grabo with painstaking advice and unflagging support, and George Starr with valuable substantive and stylistic comments. Parts of the manuscript have been read at various stages by Charles Muscatine, John Traugott, and Simon Karlinsky, and I am grateful for their attention. To Mark Schorer I am particularly indebted, not only for his sympathetic interest and illuminating criticism, but also for the inspiration provided by his kindness and gentleness of spirit. Finally I wish to thank my mother for her faith in my abilities.

I

INTRODUCTION
The Art Theme
or the Allusion of Reality

THIS STUDY grew from a delight in Nabokov's language and sense of humor, and evolved into a thematic exposition of his use of artists and artistry. In the process of critical conversion many stylistic, comic, and psychological elements had to be slighted or even omitted. Yet, at the risk of reductionism and monomania, an examination of the theme of art seemed to bring together many essential characteristics of Nabokov's novels; reflections, doublings, pedantic nostalgia, parodic seriousness, madness and perversion, death and timelessness, all touch on, though are not encompassed by, the theme of art. The relationship of these motifs to art is necessarily more subtle, complex, and moving in its indigenous fictional context than in the critical vacuum. But the critic, like Humbert, has only words to play with.

Shuddering at Nabokov's wise caution ("Remember that mediocrity thrives on 'ideas.' Beware of the modish

message. Ask yourself if the symbol you have detected
is not your own footprint. Ignore allegories. By all means
place the 'how' above the 'what' but do not let it be
confused with the 'so what' "),[1] I have several admissions
to make. The "idea" of this book is that the various levels
of "reality" in Nabokov's novels are best seen in the
perspective of the game of artifice (*realistic*, *sexual*,
American, *academic*, etc., being but different modes of
presenting illusion). My "modish message" is that in
varied forms and strange ways all of Nabokov's novels
are about art (a narrow theme if one understands art to
be separate from *reality*, *sex*, *America*, and *academe*).
This sounds allegorical, but in the footsteps of Van Veen
I would like to propose a theory of allegory which grants
the prior and superior existence of language to ideas of
what that language is about. Although several of Nabokov's critics have recognized that his novels are "about
art," or "about writing novels,"[2] and this recognition has

---

[1] Quoted in "An Interview with Vladimir Nabokov," conducted
by Alfred Appel, Jr., *Wisconsin Studies in Contemporary Literature*, VIII (1967), 133; reprinted in the anthology edited by L. S.
Dembo, *Nabokov: The Man and His Work* (Madison and London:
The University of Wisconsin Press, 1967), pp. 22–23.

[2] Foremost among these critics is Vladislav Khodasevich, whose
brilliant essay on Nabokov's early fiction has been partially reprinted in *Tri-Quarterly*, 17 (Winter, 1970), 96–101. Andrew Field's
Nabokov: His Life in Art (Boston, Toronto: Little, Brown and Co.,
1967) is consistently interesting and illuminating, and his treatment of the Nabokov canon is both comprehensive and imaginative. But his readings of the individual novels are often too sketchy,
with frequent unexplained assertions and occasional unsupported
interpretations. His book is essential as a summarized compendium
of Nabokov's *oeuvre* and as a frequently suggestive starting point
for fuller analyses of the novels. (All references to Field are to
the hardcover edition.) William Woodin Rowe's *Nabokov's Deceptive World* (New York: New York University Press, 1971) is split
between a useful study of Nabokov's language and an em-
barrassingly far-fetched examination of alleged sexual puns and
relationships.

also been widely applied to writers like Robbe-Grillet, Borges, Proust, etc., the justification for my study is that the "how" of this idea has been approached in an overly general, sketchy, or quirky manner.

Of course a work of art is inevitably a rendering of emotion, observation, and philosophical speculation in aesthetic terms, or at least in an aesthetic realm. In Nabokov's case it is not that the action or characters of a novel "stand for" or "represent" the writing of a novel or the figure of the artist, but that certain descriptions of experience, character, or emotion illuminate and approximate artistic creation. Though depicted through the medium of creative prose, and frequently compared to the process of creation, Nabokovian characters, plots, and emotions are not mere dramatizations of "ideas"

Page Stegner's *Escape into Aesthetics* (New York: The Dial Press, 1966) centers around the thesis that Nabokov regards art and private passion as an "escape" from the sordidness of external reality to a world of beauty and imagination. Stegner has many fine perceptions and a grasp of the working of significant detail in the English novels, although I disagree with his thesis about "escape." Since for Nabokov a work of art by definition exists in a world of its own, he uses and explores sordidness as an aspect and an expression of evil or isolation within his fiction. Given the assumption that the imagined world is not an escape from oppressive "reality," but a reworking of it resulting in a parallel and independent creation, Nabokov's subject is not the conflict between art and "reality," but between different conceptions of art. For Nabokov and his characters, aesthetic patterns are not a way of escaping from the empirical world but rather a way of creating a self-contained and complete world. When the characters attempt to escape from their aesthetically created selves and circumstances, it is through shifting levels of fictional reality rather than from reality to art.

Several articles have been collected in two anthologies: L. S. Dembo (ed.), *Nabokov: The Man and His Work*, and *Tri-Quarterly*, 17 (Winter, 1970). Alfred Appel, Jr.'s impressive introduction and annotations to *The Annotated Lolita* (New York, Toronto: McGraw-Hill Book Co., 1970) stress the theme of art and the presence of authorial patterning.

about art; rather they are self-contained worlds which incorporate and reshape the reader's conception of art. Any transformation in the reader's understanding of the nature of art and of the creative process is bound to influence his apprehension of his own imaginative and emotional experience. The paradoxical observation that Nabokov's novels constantly invite the reader's emotional participation, while insisting on the self-contained nature of the fictional world, points to the aesthetic center of his work. Emotional participation is achieved through the repetition of formal patterns. These patterns consist of details which become meaningful only in the special context of individual novels (such as the squirrel in *Pnin*, or the tri-vial design in *Bend Sinister*), thereby forming a unique universe within the work. But the reader's delight in the aesthetic recognition of the structure planted by the author, as well as the reader's assimilation of the sadness or joy associated with the repeated detail, results in a growing involvement with the texture of the fictional world.

The "idea" that Nabokov's novels are about the process of art, and that his heroes are artists in various guises, has little meaning without the rich and varied context of the individual novels. Nor is there any set of generalized themes or attitudes which can be substituted for the life-blood of the particular works. Insofar as this study has an "idea" for its thesis, it can be stated as the inductively demonstrated suggestion that Nabokov's novels are mainly concerned with the artistic imagination and consciousness. This theme can express itself in the creation of a work of art within the novel, as well as in the hero's self-conscious awareness of the total structure as artifice. Within this overall theme of artistic creation Nabokov explores the self-creating identity, defining itself through its obsession with an object of passion, or an imagined double, or a compulsively self-regarding prose style. It is not that Nabokov's heroes are all allegorical artist figures,[3] but that each character and plot is a study in the permutations of perception, sensibility, and imagination brought into contact with love, insanity, perversion, and death.

The sequence of the chapters was determined by thematic and structural considerations, rather than by chronology. The merging of two seemingly separate sensibilities into a single artistic consciousness, in *The Real Life of Sebastian Knight* (1941), foreshadows the exploration of the paradoxes within the artist and his dissolution into another self in *Pale Fire* (1962). The "realistic" setting of *Lolita* (1955), and the madman-pervert hero whose obsession turns into tenderness, are echoed on a minor scale by the deliberate "lifelikeness" of *Pnin* (1957), as well as by its main character's painful and unrequited devotion to his ex-wife. The thematic pairing I make between *Bend Sinister* (1947) and *Ada* (1969) is largely a matter of the affinities between the dreamer-diarist-philosopher Krug, with his speculations on time, and the writer-philosopher-lover Van Veen. The death of the main characters in *Ada*, as in *Bend Sinister*, flows into the finished artwork, reinforcing a theory of time based on a timeless, metaphoric perception of experience. The order of the chapters seemed to provide

[3] For example, Field's interpretation of *Laughter in the Dark* applies the art-formula in an oversimplified way: "[The novel is] about three failed artists," Kretschmar is a bad artist, Axel a corrupted one, and Margot an untalented though innocuous one (p. 163). Such loose readings of the artist-figure theme render its specific qualities almost meaningless. While Axel the caricaturist is indeed a perverted artist like Quilty, the figures of Kretschmar and Margot are distorted rather than illuminated if we regard them as primarily artist figures. Rather, the latter two characters are presented as consciously exploited fictional stereotypes, as the products of different methods of artistic technique.

thematic linking within the different types of authorial manipulation, while allowing for the unique qualities of each work.

Since each Nabokov novel discloses a different pattern of artistry, my stress is on the individual presentations of this theme, rather than on the general principles or abstractions exemplified by its use. The six English novels yield remarkable variations in their overall design, and Nabokov's other works reveal further variations and unique landmarks (with some inevitable similarities). Rather than simply focusing on the most apparently "artificial" of his novels (in which case *The Gift, Invitation to a Beheading, King, Queen and Knave* would have comprised a more homogeneous group), I was interested in the range and degrees of artifice manifested in such seemingly "realistic" works as *Lolita* and *Pnin*, as well as in the thematic continuities within the works conceived in English. Although *Speak, Memory* has important affinities with the novels both stylistically and structurally, it is nevertheless dictated by factual rather than fictional events. Therefore the characteristic Nabokovian devices of work-within-the work, doubling, distorted reflections, and the parodic teasing of the reader occur, if at all, within the necessities of the autobiographical framework.

To put it another way, *Speak, Memory* is artificial but not novelistic, whereas Nabokov's fiction is both. I would argue that a full awareness of the riches of Nabokov's novels involves an appreciation of the unexpected, "made-up" playfulness of the plot and characterization: artifice is the mode into which the imagined sequences are placed. My study emphasizes the workings of artifice, but the implicit delight of the novels springs from the mannered plots and characters shifting in "realistic" density and direction when visibly manipulated. In *Speak, Memory*, the novelistic qualities often prominent in the mood, the setting, or the arrangement of episodes are in the service of recreating a world, rather than imagining a fictional one. In the novels Fate is Nabokov's creature (Aubrey and Gradus both merge in the mirror of Sudarg), while in the autobiography fate can be only chronicled, not manipulated.

Many of the studies concerned with Nabokov's novels are either trapped in conventional topics of novel criticism (such as point of view, consistency of characterization, realistic observation, and symbolic coherence), or in bare descriptions of the obvious plot movements. But Nabokov's work eludes traditional rubrics of interpretation either through use of parody or conscious disregard, and the novels toy with numerous subjects and plot possibilities without being "about" any of them. The novels are "about art" only in the loose sense of existing in a deliberately artificial world, and being constructed according to techniques and structural rules which are explicitly designed to suggest the interior process of creation rather than the exterior world of empirical objects.

My extended explications focus on Nabokov's treatment of the theme of art, the artist's relation to his work, and the manifestations of the artistic consciousness. This focus has led me to consider the specific structural form of each novel as seen through the movement of its recurring motifs, and to speculate about the way the various structural forms mirror and contain different types of artistic creation. Each of the novels I analyze can be viewed as a unique network of objects, images, and allusions—the Nabokovian points of reference which create a live fictional world. These networks are allegories of artistic creation in the sense that they make us aware of the act of imagining a reflected and inverted universe. Nabokov locks his characters into prisons or cages of various shapes and designs; the author and the reader share a perception of the patterns invisible to the characters within.

The pattern may be one of recurring detail, motif, or stylistic technique, sometimes forming an overall pursuit for the reality of art, as in *Lolita* and *Ada*. The movement and manipulation of emotional experience through pattern is one of the main interests of each novel. As characters are turned toward different aspects of fictional technique by the omniscient narrator, we feel the narrator self-consciously embroidering the figures of his magic carpet. Thus in the development of the aesthetic experience, the theme or fabric is that of artistic reality; but both the shape of the experience itself, and the method of development, are different in each novel. The unfolding drama of pursuit, and the web of references, constitute perhaps the most distinctive and pleasurable excitements for the reader of Nabokov. Nabokov experiments with vitally new forms of conceiving and executing the presentation of the artist's relation to art: the ordinary fictional character's relation to the extraordinarily patterned world of art (*Pnin*); the madman's quest for ecstasy and his discovery of an artistic pattern through love (*Lolita*); the search for an artistic identity (*Sebastian Knight*); the structure built on the self-annihilating and regenerative nature of artistic creation (*Pale Fire*); the linked circles of creation between main character and author (*Bend Sinister*); and the artist's use of subjective temporal reality and his own sensuality to chronicle narrative recurrences (*Ada*).[4]

---

[4] *Pnin* (Garden City: Doubleday and Co., 1957); *Lolita* (New York: Crest Paperback, 1962); *The Real Life of Sebastian Knight* (Norfolk: New Directions, 1941); *Pale Fire* (New York: G. P. Putnam's Sons, 1962); *Bend Sinister* (London: Corgi Books, 1962); *Ada* (New York and Toronto: McGraw-Hill Book Co., 1969). All references, unless otherwise indicated, will be to these editions.

Although each novel creates its own sense of reality, Nabokov's fictional world is not monolithic. The author constantly invades and overturns the illusion of reality. His interruptions are not mere asides, necessary explanations, or digressions; they are a crucial element in the total design. Insofar as each work is primarily concerned with imagination and consciousness, the joy of awareness and the abandonment to the ecstasy of perception are perpetually threatened by destruction. The author's intrusions are reminders of the perilously provisional nature of the fictional web. These reminders and breaks in the conventional surface deprive the fiction of its lifelike depth, and create an abyss where the fictional depth had been.

Nabokov's interruptions and shifting guises are often playful exposures of the reader's banal expectations of art as a mirror of reality with consistent, "lifelike" details. The authorial intrusions are frequently distorted echoes and parodies of novelistic conventions, as well as verbal and literary games which assert the presence of the writer behind the artifact. But the most complicated and emotionally moving function of these rents in fictional illusion is to produce a frightening chasm beneath the pleasures of language, sensuous awareness, and artistic creation. The deliberate hollowness beneath the lacquered surface is profoundly disturbing to the reader precisely because it is the aesthetic equivalent to the Nabokovian horror of the state of nonbeing where human perception is annihilated. In creating a chasm of discontinuities within his fiction, the writer can both approximate the dread of being shut off from the keen pleasures of consciousness and exercise a kind of control over death and loss through artistic assertion. In the latter sense, death becomes a problem in fictional representation, a "question of style," as the author observes

toward the end of *Bend Sinister* (p. 222). In *Pale Fire*,
John Shade exemplifies this dual awareness in his speculation that there are celestial players directing human
affairs and frustrating the artistic aspiration for immortality, and in his triumph over mortality through the
weaving of a unique game of death.

Nabokov's private references often parody conventional literary ones. These parodies are intermittent, discontinuous, often shifting their target from specific works
to generic characteristics: in *Sebastian Knight* the fictional autobiography; in *Pnin* the academic/victim novel;
in *Pale Fire* critical exegesis; in *Bend Sinister* political
allegory; in *Lolita* the erotic memoir; in *Ada* the family
chronicle. The literary patterns are often coupled with a
sporadic representation of "realistic" backgrounds: the
Americana of *Pnin*, *Lolita*, and *Pale Fire*; the middle-class
Berlin life in *Laughter in the Dark*; the daily details in
the papier-maché prison in *Invitation to a Beheading*; the
factual information about Sebastian in *Sebastian Knight*;
the genealogy and Ardis' geography in *Ada*. But the realistic inserts, like the parodic winks at literary conventions,
are merely springboards for the imaginative fancies.

It is impossible to generalize about the form of Nabokov's works, except to note that each is a formalistic
departure from fictional conventions. The particular
shape of each work involves the reader in an effort of
disentangling the sham pattern from the meaningful one,
the banal clues planted for the "inimical reader" from
the delicate "cryptograms" supplied for the careful re-
reader. The implications and use of chess in Nabokov's
novels have been noted by several critics.[5] A striking
analogue for Nabokov's fictional composition is sug-

[5] The most interesting, although rather unsympathetic, treatment of the theme is Strother B. Purdy's "Solus Rex: Nabokov and
the Chess Novel," *Modern Fiction Studies*, 14 (1968), 379–395.

gested in his description of a chess problem in *Speak, Memory:*

> It was meant for the delectation of the very expert solver. The unsophisticated might miss the point of the problem entirely, and discover its fairly simple, "thetic" solution without having passed through the pleasurable torments prepared for the sophisticated one. The latter would start by falling for an illusory pattern of play based on a fashionable avant-garde theme . . . which the composer had taken the greatest pains to "plant." The pleasant experience of the roundabout route (strange landscapes, gongs, tigers, exotic customs, the thrice-repeated circuit of a newly married couple around the sacred fire of an earthen brazier) would amply reward him for the misery of the deceit, and after that, his arrival at the simple key-move would provide him with a synthesis of poignant artistic delight. (Pp. 221–222.)

The "fashionable avant-garde theme" may be Humbert's passion for nymphets, Kinbote's interest in faunlets (and *Pale Fire*'s critical explications), the soul-searching literary biography of *Sebastian Knight*, or even the delightful but incidental "academic" details of *Pnin*. The "fairly simple" resolution is "artistic" in several ways: not only in producing a sensation of discovery akin to artistic creation, but also in leading us back to the theme of art (artistic composition, its possible perversions, its dangers of dislocation and madness, and often the figure and personality of the artist himself).

Nabokovian characters have intermittent, temporary personalities brought to life by a trick of lighting, by a transitory sleight-of-hand. This deliberately discontinuous technique of characterization implies that the self is alive only when observed and observing. Without the intense awareness and vividness conferred by imaginative concentration, the self becomes static, one-dimensional, and eventually withers away. Nabokov's characters exist only at moments when their "reality" is colored in on the sketched pattern; their solidity is illusory, a miracle of language which is emphasized by the return of the authorial voice and the reminder of the novelistic technique employed in the characterization. Character is McFate.

The anagrams, recurrent details, and playful allusions reinforce the impression of Nabokovian structure as an intellectually created, ostentatiously artificial form. Inconsistent and discontinuous characters are a part of this structure, merging with whimsical detail and playful involutions of plot. The verbal and literary games are not merely decorative additions to the form and meaning of Nabokov's novels, as has been suggested in connection with *Ada*.[6] The details of surface texture embody and express the meaning; it is through these details that the artistic consciousness constructs its imaginary world. The exploration of the imagination, of the varieties of artistic techniques, and of the mysteries of human psychology is recorded through the intricacies of deliberate artifice. The search for pattern is both chronicled by and projected onto the made-up world of self-conscious literary games. Since this world is an interior mirror of the artist's imagination as filtered through his manipulation of novelistic tools, the surface texture is the most telling reflection of a personal vision.

[6] Cf. Robert Alter, "Nabokov's Ardor," *Commentary*, XLVIII (August, 1969), 50: "Fortunately, the code-games and allusions in *Ada* are merely pointers to the peculiar nature of the novel's imaginative richness, which does not finally depend on the clues."

II

SEBASTIAN KNIGHT
The Oneness of Perception

SEBASTIAN KNIGHT deliberately casts a distorted shadow of its proposed literary projects. The narrator, V., purports to write a biography of his dead half-brother, Sebastian Knight. The product of V.'s search is not the biography but the quest for it; not Sebastian's "real life," but Sebastian's fictional existence. V.'s technique of arranging the events of Sebastian's life is itself artistic: "My quest had developed its own magic and logic . . . it had gradually grown into a dream, that quest, using the pattern of reality for the weaving of its own fancies" (p. 137). The novel might be titled *The Dream Life of Sebastian Knight*, the "pattern of reality" from which it constantly departs consisting of the circumstantial events of Sebastian's life, and the "fancies" being Sebastian's beautiful novels filtered through V.'s narration. It becomes increasingly clear that the "real life" of Sebastian was contained not in external circumstances but in his writings; and since these writings exist for us in V.'s retelling of them, Sebastian lives in V. who has recreated his brother's artistic and personal life in his own imagination. Thus "real" is gradually defined as the living, growing shadow of a life in prose, a shadow which engulfs the factual biography.

Once we realize the inescapable oneness of Sebastian and V., the "literary trick" element of the novel becomes obvious. *Sebastian Knight* leads toward a discovery, and to the superficial eye the discovery is contained in V.'s ingenuously wide-eyed revelation, on the last page of the novel, "that the soul is but a manner of being—not a constant state—that any soul may be yours, if you find and follow its undulations. The hereafter may be the full ability of consciously living in any chosen soul, in any number of souls, all of them unconscious of their interchangeable burden, Thus—I am Sebastian Knight. . . . I am Sebastian, or Sebastian is I, or perhaps we both are someone whom neither of us knows" (pp. 204–205). If we read "art" for "the hereafter," and Vladimir Nabokov for the "someone" whom neither V. nor Sebastian "knows," we have gained an essential insight into the technique of the novel.

But this ending is a "trick" in the sense that it tells us something we have guessed all along, and the more astonishing and central discovery is hidden elsewhere in the book. The merging of Sebastian and V., and their ultimate dissolution in an omniscient authorial presence, is the culmination of one of the two basic thematic strands in the novel: the concern with methods of fictional composition. What all the different methods have in common is the author's "conscious" presence in all the "souls" (i.e., characters) of his novel. *Dead Souls* (one of Nabokov's favorite novels, specifically mentioned by V.) can be literally applied to Nabokovian characters, in the

sense that we are constantly reminded that the only existence they possess is given to them by the author, so
that they are no more than reflections of the artistic preoccupation with different motifs.)

The other strand of *Sebastian Knight*, which gently
curves around the concern with methods of fictional composition, is the search for the precise relationship between
perception and imagination. The "secret" of this relationship is the real discovery of *Sebastian Knight*, born of the
joint mode of two of Sebastian's novels: his first and his
last. "Two modes of his life question each other and the
answer is his life itself, and that is the nearest one ever
can approach a human truth" (p. 137), V. tells us. The
modes of Sebastian's life are artistic ones, "the man is the
book" (p. 175), and the "human truth" is the anguished
vision of beauty sliding into the past, but recoverable
through an act of imagination.

The mosaics of *Sebastian Knight* are interlocking; a
composition maneuvered by an omniscient author who
plants details and characters with delicate but deliberately observable gestures. The "true conflict," Nabokov
tells us, is always between author and reader, between
the author's unique solutions to "games of his own invention" (p. 181) and the reader's habitual preconcep-
tions about fiction. All of Nabokov's figures in *Sebastian
Knight* are nonrealistic, though in varying degrees, and
the shadings of their dimensions create a fantasy world
where detail reflects on other detail, with the final product
mirroring not reality, but itself. "They are, these lives,
but commentaries to the main subject" (p. 175), and the
main subject is more than a technical problem, or a proper
aesthetic solution: it is the combination of literary composition with patterns of human fate, leading to moments
of "curiosity, tenderness, kindness, ecstasy." Sebastian's
own novels are small clusters of such moments, individual

windows to the soul of the total novel. They are beautiful puddles (one of Nabokov's recurrent images) whose reflection is picked up by the mirror of the novel itself, which in turn reflects the author's imagination.

Theme and method often become slightly distorted in this process of multiple mirroring, but the end product is not a statement about the emptiness of illusion. Rather, the collective reflections reinforce the "synthesized spirality" of human perception. Each spiral ascends to a higher plane of imagination. One of the central insights in Nabokov's *Speak, Memory* is that "in the spiral form, the circle, uncoiled, unwound, has ceased to be vicious; it has been set free" (p. 204). I regard each of Sebastian's novels within *The Real Life of Sebastian Knight* as small spirals whose joint effect is to impart a "truth" about the oneness of human perception.

Sebastian's first novel, *The Prismatic Bezel*, is "based cunningly on certain tricks of the literary trade," such as the detective story, the use of a "medley of people in a limited space," "the boarding-house motif," and the "country-house motif." Each of these parodies is employed as a "springboard for leaping into the highest region of serious emotion" (pp. 91–95). *The Prismatic Bezel* parodies different styles and techniques, as well as themes, but exploits the parody as a means of enforcing the shifting and illusory nature of "reality." It is well for us to remember that "bezel" is defined as (1) the sloping edge of a chisel or other cutting tool, (2) the oblique faces of a brilliant-cut gem, and (3) the grooved ring or rim holding a gem or crystal in its setting. Thus "bezel" refers simultaneously to the tool (i.e., method), the gem (i.e., the theme), and that which holds the gem in place (the style).

"The essential oneness" of literary technique is insisted on in all Nabokov novels. Parody, one of Nabokov's favorite methods, serves to startle the reader into an awareness that his comfortable notions of fiction and "reality" are about to be exploded. The theme of the banality of stock characters and situations is only the starting point. The precise, lucid, uniquely glinting style points to the more important theme: that a vision of beauty can be achieved through a freedom from trite pre-conceptions and ready-made metaphors. The "plot" of *The Prismatic Bezel* demonstrates the progression toward this kind of emotional and intellectual freedom. Starting with a murder in a boarding-house, "something in the story begins to shift"; all the lodgers are revealed to be connected with each other, and the story is transposed to a country-house. In this new setting the technique be-comes "realistic," "the lives of the characters shine forth with a real and human significance." But "realism" turns out to be merely an alternate method of composition, and "at the very moment when the reader feels quite safe in an atmosphere of pleasurable reality," the scene shifts again, and the parody of the detective story is resumed. But the corpse has disappeared, and a harmless "passer-by" removes his disguise and reveals himself to be the man supposed murdered. His explanation for the mas-querade, "one dislikes being murdered," is the statement of the author himself, who refuses to refine himself out of existence, who insists on upsetting the fictional illu-sion, who appears in order to put literary conventions in a diminished perspective.

The Prismatic Bezel, like all of Nabokov's own novels, is "not the painting of a landscape, but the painting of different ways of painting a certain landscape" (p. 95). The occupation of the man who "dislikes being mur-dered" is given as "art-dealer." To "deal" in art means to experiment in different manners of presenting fictional "reality." If the soul is but a "manner of being," the creation of different souls is but the artistic projection of various manners of being. V.'s final, highest estimate of *The Doubtful Asphodel*, Sebastian's last novel, is: "I like its manners" (p. 182).

The "certain landscape" of *The Prismatic Bezel* (a man supposed dead, the search for the killer, the shift to the country-house, the essential connection between all the characters, and the unmasking of the "art-dealer") is refracted by the overall outline of *Sebastian Knight*. V. searches for his own identity through clues he has about the life of his dead brother. These clues include Sebastian's "first adolescent romance," which V. depicts in terms of an incomplete dramatic scene: "The curtain rises and a Russian summer landscape is disclosed: . . . the painter has not yet filled in the white space [of the girl] except for a thin sunburnt arm" (pp. 137–138). Sebastian's later romance with Clare Bishop is described as "alliterative" and joyful, but finally dead because its edges grew "hazy" (p. 113). The "formula" of "another woman" leads V.'s detective search to a country-house where his "manner" changes (p. 154). But the *femme fatale* theme peters out, and the summarized details of *The Doubtful Asphodel* stress the fact that all the disparate characters in Sebastian's life are intimately related to each other through being fictional props in the same plot. Finally, the dead man is resurrected ("I am Sebastian") in the narrator, and both are revealed to be aspects of the conjuring art-dealer, Nabokov.

But just as *The Prismatic Bezel* parodies detective stories whose predictable search for the real killer ends in an easily anticipated discovery, *Sebastian Knight* parodies stories of literary detection which conclude with the unmasking of the real author behind the narrator. Although *Sebastian Knight* ostensibly follows this literary trail, the object of the search is not the artist himself, but rather the meaning of his art. As Nabokov warns in the Afterword to *Lolita*: "If you do not watch out, the real murderer may turn out to be, to the fan's disgust, artistic originality." Artistic originality is contained in no single idea or "word," as V. naively expects in his perusal of *The Doubtful Asphodel*, but in the "combination of the parts," in the interwoven phrases, startling images, and teasing details. Sebastian "had no use for ready-made phrases because the things he wanted to say were of an exceptional build and he knew moreover that no real idea can be said to exist without the words made to mea-sure . . . the words lurking afar were not empty shells as they seemed, but were only waiting for the thought they already concealed to set them aflame and in motion" (p. 84).

By parodying prevalent literary conventions the author questions the reader's assumptions about literature, and by using these parodies as "springboards" he surprises and corrects these assumptions by a burst of literary originality. The "manner" of *The Prismatic Bezel* is paro-dic, that of *The Doubtful Asphodel* one of "serious emo-tion," and *The Real Life of Sebastian Knight* utilizes both modes. Sebastian's other works suggest alternate meth-ods and themes, other ways of arriving at the "secret" relationship between the words and the thought em-bodied in them. The discovery of *Sebastian Knight* is that the secret is decipherable; it lurks not behind the author's mask but within the colored spirals of the combinations and recombinations of "the certain landscape" of his style.

Sebastian's second novel, *Success*, is described as one plane "higher" than the first, "for, if his first novel is based on methods of literary composition—the second one deals mainly with methods of human fate" (p. 95). Given the "formula" of two people who meet and live

happily "ever after," the novel sets out to examine how
the formula is arrived at. The justification for this task is
"the fundamental assumption that an author is able to
discover anything he may want to know about his characters, such capacity being limited only by the manner
and purpose of his selection insofar as it ought to be not
a haphazard jumble of worthless details but a definite
and methodical quest" (pp. 95–96). In the course of his
research Sebastian concludes that outward circumstances
(i.e., objective reality) are not a causal part of human fate,
they are no more than "fixed points." He does not tell us
what the methods of human fate are, except that these
methods succeed (hence the title *Success*) "by such delicate machinations that not the merest click is audible
when at last the two are brought together" (p. 98). This
suggests the important assumption that "fate" is a result
of subtle authorial manipulation, and literary techniques
are a means of creating and refining rather than repro-
ducing the patterns of human fate. But only by perfecting
the uniqueness and freshness of literary composition can
a writer hope to discover his particular relation to circum-
stance and fate. The methods of fate are open to the
artistic sensibility because these methods can be arranged
through the "delicate machinations" of fictional creation.[1]
For Nabokov, fate lurks in the turns of prose style,

---

[1] At the end of Nabokov's novel *The Gift*, the hero recapitulates the plot of the entire novel in his musings about "fate's
methods," and contemplates writing his own novel of how he
happened to meet the girl he will live with: "The first attempt to
bring us together was crude and heavy! . . . The idea lacked sub-
tlety: to have us meet through Lorentz's wife. . . . But at this
point fate blundered: the medium chosen was wrong. . . . [Finally]
I myself don't know why but the maneuver worked . . . it began
with reckless impetuosity and ended with the finest of finishing
touches. Now isn't that the plot for a remarkable novel? What
a theme! But it must be built up, curtained, surrounded by dense
life. . . ." (New York: G. P. Putnam's Sons, 1963), pp. 375–376.

revealing the destiny the writer has prepared for his puppets.

The narrator's composition of his half-brother's life is full of details which may seem haphazard at first reading, but fall into a methodical pattern designed to reveal the essence of Sebastian's artistry. For example, Sebastian's next work is a collection of three short stories, "The Funny Mountain," "Albinos in Black," and "The Back of the Moon." While composing "The Funny Mountain," he is interrupted by a "meek little man" who is "waiting" to see him. A paragraph later we are told that "The Back of the Moon" has a "delightful character," a "meek little man waiting for a train," who is the "most alive of Sebastian's creatures" (pp. 103–104). Later, after the narrator has failed to get the names of the women who had a possible connection with Sebastian, "a little man," complete with all the physical characteristics of the fictional character in "The Back of the Moon," appears, procures the names for him, and provides him with advice: "You can't see de odder side of de moon. Please don't search de woman'" (p. 132).[2]

There are numerous other echoes in connection with this character, who is named Siller in Sebastian's story and introduces himself to V. as Silbermann. One of the passages which V. quotes from *The Prismatic Bezel* has two details which seem relevant to Siller: "A policeman passed leading the night on a leash, and then paused to let it sniff at a pillar box" (p. 98), and the conjuror (bald and black-suited like Siller) saying, " 'They don't kinda like my accent, but I guess I'm going to get that turn all the same' " (p. 99). Silbermann tells V. that he deals in

[2] This recurrence is also noted in Susan Fromberg's perceptive essay, "The Unwritten Chapters in *The Real Life of Sebastian Knight*," *Modern Fiction Studies*, 13 (1967), 427–442, and in Andrew Field's *Nabokov: His Life in Art*, p. 27.

"hound-muzzles," and has been in "de police" (p. 127), and his appearance is perhaps the "turn" the conjuror gets with a revamped accent.

The appearance within the novel of a character depicted in Sebastian's short story serves to remind us that *The Real Life* exists on a receding series of fictional planes; that the action narrated by V. is no more "real" than the character created by Sebastian. The intermingling of various fictional planes, and the repetition of some clues and details in Sebastian's fiction by V.'s narrative, foreshadow the moment when V. declares: "I am Sebastian Knight."

Further mystification is provided by Sebastian's next novel, *Lost Property*, which is a kind of literary "summing up" of the journey of discovery. We are not told of its plot or technique, only of a chapter about an airplane crash in which half a dozen letters are scattered at the site. "Two of these were business letters of great importance; a third was addressed to a woman, but it began: 'Dear Mr. Mortimer, in reply to yours of the 6th inst . . .'; and the last was an envelope directed to a firm of traders with the wrong letter inside, a love letter" (p. 112). These two letters have been mixed up and put in the wrong envelopes, either by Sebastian, who wrote the chapter, or by V., who is telling us about it. But strangely, the "Mr. Mortimer" of the first letter is mentioned in the second one: "I have not been able to clinch the business I was supposed to bring 'to a satisfactory close,' as that ass Mortimer says" (p. 114). The second letter is a farewell to a mistress, and V. quotes it for its probable relevance to Sebastian's relationship with Clare. But the details of the letter ("I shall joke with the chaps at the office," the "business" with Mortimer) correspond to V.'s life; V. works in an office, and his "unsatisfactory" business meeting is recorded in the novel. The question arises

whether V. is the writer of both the narrative and the
alleged novels of Sebastian, or whether Sebastian has
created a letter written by a fictitious V. The shifting and
obscuring of identities is in part a joyous game, and ultimately testifies to the imaginative flexibility of the author,
whose consciousness encompasses both Sebastian and V.
The identity of the narrator, the subject of his project,
and the circumstances of their separate lives are placed
in a deliberately jumbled design which undermines the
"realistic" façade of V.'s tale.

Just as the letter in *Lost Property* is saying goodbye
to the mistress who made the writer happy, the outer
novel is saying goodbye to Clare, who is now being de-
serted by the plot. She is sorrowfully but inevitably left
for another theme, what the letter refers to as "the
damned formula of 'another woman'" (p. 113). When
V. attempts to find the "other woman," her first husband
describes her as if she were nothing more than a literary
motif: "You may find her in any cheap novel, she's a type,
a type" (p. 146); "a bad dream after seeing a bad cinema
film" (p. 147). And V. wonders whether a woman like that
could have interested Sebastian, whether her image was
not "too obvious," a prototype of "ready-made forms of
pleasure and hackneyed forms of distress" (p. 149).

The plausibility of the "other woman" who destroys a
man's life is thus being considered from a chiefly literary
point of view. Is it worth our while to turn to this trite
trail? But *The Real Life of Sebastian Knight* manages to
turn the "other woman" motif into an unusual quest; V.
meets a woman whose identity is almost as elusive as his
own, a woman compounded of "oldish French novels,"
whimsical, cruel, and banal. The summary of her life
dovetails with that of a conventional formula: "The men
she liked proved dismal disappointments, all women with
few exceptions were nothing but cats, and she spent the

best part of her life in trying to be happy in a world which did its best to break her" (p. 161). She embodies all the insipid stereotypes of French romances: a *femme fatale*, a woman "good as good bread" (p. 162). V.'s involvement with her reminds him of "that breathless phrase in that second-rate Maupassant story: 'I have forgotten a book' " (p. 171).

But what is no more than a conventional amorous gambit in Maupassant is a reminder for V. and for the reader, that the "other woman" formula leads away from the live center of *Sebastian Knight*. Another false literary lead is thus dropped, and V. is left to confront Sebastian's last novel. This last novel is not a repudiation of hackneyed conventions; in fact, parody plays no part in its technique at all. Having scrutinized and tested literary convention, Sebastian the artist is now disclosing the meaning of his unique vision. The process of this disclosure is itself essential; the "secret" is muted and submerged in its own details to such an extent that even V. seems to bypass it.

The "composition" of the parts, in the sequence in which V. depicts *The Doubtful Asphodel*, is characteristically Nabokovian. I think we are presented with an astonishing and lucid revelation which is the apex of the entire novel. But the revelation is couched in an oblique manner which minimizes the aura of epiphany (Nabokov again declines to employ a popular formula) and almost tricks us into believing that the revelation has not taken place. The theme of "a man dying" is extended to the book:—"The book itself is heaving and dying"; we are given details which have occurred within the action of *The Real Life*, intermingled with other details which belong to *The Doubtful Asphodel* alone. (An "asphodel" is a kind of lily whose elongated stem bears flowers on short stalks in a methodical succession toward the apex of the plant.)

Nabokov here seems to be playing with the microcosm-macrocosm convention, suggesting that Sebastian's last novel may be a reflection of the whole novel we are reading. But, as the title itself indicates, the narcissistic reflection of the lily has a correspondence to the actual flower which is at best "doubtful." V. reminds us that in the case of *The Doubtful Asphodel*, "it is not the parts that matter, it is their combinations" (p. 176). The parts themselves resemble the parts of *The Real Life of Sebastian Knight*—the chess player Schwarz, the fat Bohemian woman, the soft-lipped girl in mourning, all have their slightly distorted counterparts in the macrocosmic plot—but the combinations differ. V's narrative is concerned with both more and less than "a man dying"; and most importantly, the ending of *The Real Life of Sebastian Knight* provides us with a "secret" other than that of *The Doubtful Asphodel*.

The discovery contained in *The Doubtful Asphodel* is a fusion of emotional and artistic "truth" which illuminates an intrinsic pattern similar to that perceived by Shade in *Pale Fire:*

. . . it was like a traveller realizing that the wild country he surveys is not an accidental assembly of natural phenomena, but the page in a book where these mountains and forests, and fields, and rivers are disposed in such a way as to form a coherent sentence; the vowel of a lake fusing with the consonant of a sibilant slope; . . . Thus the traveller spells the landscape and its sense is disclosed, and likewise, the intricate pattern of human life turns out to be monogrammatic, now quite clear to the inner eye disentangling the interwoven letters. (P. 179.)

The pattern of human life is made intelligible by the precise artistic expression of that pattern; methods of com-

position and methods of fate are disclosed in the act of
literary creation. For the reader they are disclosed in the
act of reading, when he is provided with a new "painting"
of the landscape of reality. "The answer to all questions
of life and death, 'the absolute solution' was written all
over the world he had known: . . . the greatest surprise
being perhaps that in the course of one's earthly existence, with one's brain encompassed by an iron ring, by
the close-fitting dream of one's own personality—one
had not made by chance that simple mental jerk, which
would have set free imprisoned thought and granted it
the great understanding" (pp. 178–179).

Sebastian, the artist, suddenly understands that his
life has meaning only in terms of his art; that "the close-
fitting dream of his own personality" has restricted him
from perceiving the possibilities for a dazzling freedom of
the imagination. A "simple mental jerk" frees the artist
from the "iron ring" of a single personality, and allows
his life to flow into fictional characters who are unlike
him. The pleasure and absorption in fictional characters
who are distant and dissimilar from us is the great "secret" and discovery of art. The ability to create this sensation of simultaneous distance and absorption is the
"solution" to the artist's quest; Sebastian has given us
the "truth" to this work of art, to this "problem" of
meaning. Thus V.'s final revelation about the interchange-
ability of souls is really part of the more important disclosure in *The Doubtful Asphodel*, that a "simple mental
jerk" can free one from the confines of space and time—
in short, from the physical and emotional "reality" of a
single personality. This artistic and psychological statement is basic to Nabokov's art: the vision attained
through alienation from one's personality, the glimpse of
beauty which the perverted Humbert, the exiled Pnin, the

mad Kinbote gain through their partial acquisition of imaginary roles.

But the revelations are momentary and ever-changing. Each art work, often even each chapter and paragraph, has its own secret to yield. V., who has just told us about the above-quoted passages in *The Doubtful Asphodel*, seems to be searching for another secret, perhaps a single "word" which is never given because the protagonist dies at a crucial moment. But V.'s sense of a hovering answer remains, and he says of *The Doubtful Asphodel*: "I sometimes feel when I turn the pages of Sebastian's masterpiece that the 'absolute solution' is there, somewhere, concealed in some passage I have read too hastily, or that it is intertwined with other words whose familiar guise deceived me. I don't know any other book that gives one this special sensation, and perhaps this was the author's special intention" (p. 180). The feeling we have as readers—that V. has indeed missed the "solution" by reading hastily or imperceptively—adds to the comic nature of his amateurish quest, but also reminds us that there may be other secrets, other imaginative freedoms, which will solve different problems of artistic composition and illuminate other patterns of human fate.

Another dream quest, again pointing to the solution contained in Sebastian's artistry, occurs in V.'s "singularly unpleasant dream" about his half-brother. Sebastian appears to him, wearing "a black glove on his left hand," which he takes off, spilling "a number of tiny hands," representing the sinister manipulative capacity of the artist. V. misses the chance to hear the solution from Sebastian; he is paralyzed by his own terror and the armor of a single personality, "the sovereignty of daily platitudes over the delicate revelations of a dream" (p. 190). But *The Doubtful Asphodel*'s suggestion of a free-

dom from such platitudes through the originality of artistic creation is reasserted by the final action of the novel.
The "tiny hands" of the author further dramatize the
finding of Sebastian's last novel.

We have been told that the theme of *The Doubtful
Asphodel*, the partial reflection of *Sebastian Knight*, is
that

a man is dying: you feel him sinking throughout the book;
his thought and memories pervade the whole with greater or
lesser distinction. . . . He is the hero of the tale; but whereas
the lives of other people in the book seem perfectly realistic
(or at least realistic in a Knightian sense), the reader is kept
ignorant as to who the dying man is. . . . The man is the book,
the book itself is heaving and dying, and drawing up a
ghostly knee. (P. 175.)

If "the man is the book," then the man, the hero of the
novel, contains the "other people" who may be momentarily given an air of reality, but ultimately fade back into
the mind of the hero, which in turn is identified as part
of the imagination of the author.* One of Sebastian's
important findings is that " 'all things belong to the same
order of things, for such is the oneness of human perception, the oneness of individuality, the oneness of matter, whatever matter may be. The only real number is one,
the rest are mere repetition' " (p. 105). In terms of artistic technique, this statement means that regardless of the
ostensible "point of view" of any given passage, the
speaker is always, inescapably, the author. At the end
of an interview with Goodman, the slick author of a rival

---

* The fact that Sebastian was planning to write a fictitious biography, his exclamation that he is not dead, the narcissistic portrait in which he seems to be looking at the reflection of his other
self, and the manipulative little hands hint at Sebastian's possible
authorship of his own biography. As in *Bend Sinister*, the imaginative circles merge and diverge, the chronology of details is teasingly jumbled, and the autonomy of the fictional artist is suggested
but interrupted by a larger consciousness.

biography of Sebastian, V. "pockets" the "black mask" which Goodman has been wearing, and remarks that "it might come in usefully on some other occasion" (p. 59).[3] This event is another reminder that the parts allotted to various characters in *Sebastian Knight* are only temporary roles involving a "black mask" which is reusable. It is perhaps this same device which V.'s final declaration alludes to: "I cannot get out of my part: Sebastian's mask clings to my face" (p. 205).

"The only real number is one," as a psychological statement, is an essential part of the novel, and embodies the truth about the impact of life and art. We understand experience only through our perception of its personal significance, just as we understand art only when we grasp the nature and fittingness of its arranged details tending toward a completed design. For Nabokov, psychological understanding is "one" with artistic appreciation; when the reader feels that a work of art is meaningful for him, he will see how it has been rendered meaningful. Used in this sense, the word "psychology" is not blasphemous for Nabokov; as he writes in the Foreword to *The Eye*: "A serious psychologist . . . may distinguish through my rain-sparkling cryptograms a world of soul dissolution." In the case of *The Eye*, the

---

[3] Goodman is a version of the recurrent Nabokovian villain-hack whose insensitivity and trite prose style are viewed with scorn and derision. I can find no support in *Sebastian Knight* for Dabney Stuart's contention that V. employs the same techniques as Goodman, that Goodman's approach yields a serious "truth" about Sebastian which V. refuses to recognize out of vanity. Stuart reads the ending ("I am Sebastian . . . ," etc.) as an affirmation of the impossibility of knowing, though such a reading seems to me to conflict with the movement and design of the novel. What V. finds out in the process of the narrative is precisely a way of knowing which yields emotional freedom and aesthetic pleasure. Cf. Dabney Stuart, "*The Real Life of Sebastian Knight*: Angles of Perception," *Modern Language Quarterly*, 29 (1968), 312–328.

hero exists only insofar as he is mirrored by other souls. In *Sebastian Knight*, the life and commentary of V. exist in order to surround Sebastian's works with an illusion of reality. These works in turn reflect the "number one," the author and finally the reader; they are mirrors to perception.

The primacy of the subjective self in assigning meaning to experience is illustrated by two similar incidents in the novel, which act partly as repeated frames to the total work. The first occurs in the beginning of *Sebastian Knight*, and describes Sebastian's visit to a pension where he thinks his adored mother had died thirteen years before. The idea of her presence at the place produces a sense of emotional revelation: "Gradually I worked myself into such a state that for a moment the pink and green seemed to shimmer and float as if seen through a veil of mist" (p. 19). Later he finds out that he had gone to the wrong town. Toward the end of the novel, when V. receives news that Sebastian is dying, he rushes to the sanatorium, and sits by what he had been told is his half-brother's bedside. The emotion he experiences changes his attitude toward Sebastian; for the first time he realizes the "warm flow" of "the wave of love" which transfigures their relationship. Afterwards he is told that it was the wrong bedside, and that Sebastian had died the day before. But in both incidents, it was not the object of emotion which precipitated the change, but rather the psychological predilection of the beholder. Empirical reality was ancillary to emotional illusion. The "secret" which unlocked the feeling lay in the sudden perception of a meaningful pattern. The quest for Sebastian's identity is resolved by V.'s finding and duplicating the artistic process which weaves its own reality. In this duplication V. and Sebastian become one.

III

PALE FIRE
*Refracted
Shades of the Poet*

PALE FIRE contains two seemingly separate works of art:
Shade's poem and Kinbote's commentary. The poet and
the mad commentator are ostensibly distinct personalities; Shade's poem about his everyday life, his speculations on death, art, and the hereafter, appear to be in
contrast to Kinbote's pitiful intrigues, ludicrous literary
sensitivity, maudlin religiosity, and grandiose fantasy-
life. But the separation into autonomous characters—
Shade, Kinbote, Gradus—is only apparent. The primary
subject of *Pale Fire* is the emotional-stylistic exploration
of the artist's imagination both contemplating death and
experiencing it through self-willed creative annihilation.
Shade, I maintain, has perpetrated his own "stylistic"
death within the novel, and he has then given us a new
aspect of himself in the guise of another soul and another
artwork (Kinbote and the commentary).

The structural and thematic interpretations of *Pale Fire*

which I am proposing have their counterparts elsewhere in Nabokov's writings. Kinbote's editing of Shade's poem is analogous to V.'s "biography" of his half-brother Sebastian Knight. In both cases the commentary surrounds and almost engulfs the artwork within the novels; both commentators, moreover, use the "pattern of reality for the weaving of [their] own fancies." Although there are obvious differences in characterization between Kinbote and V., the merging of the two main characters in *Sebastian Knight*, the "biography's" emphasis on the "oneness of human perception," and the revelation—in Sebastian's *The Doubtful Asphodel*—that the creative artist can shrug off the "close-fitting dream of his own personality," all suggest resemblances to *Pale Fire*'s complex pattern. Death represented as self-willed artistic annihilation has its echoes elsewhere in Nabokov's work. At the end of *Bend Sinister*, the author tells us that his main character finds out "that death was but a question of style" (p. 222). In "The Room," the speaker observes that

> A poet's death is, after all,
> A question of technique, a neat
> Enjambment, a melodic fall.[1]

In *The Real Life of Sebastian Knight*, V. exults in the thought that "the hereafter may be the full ability of consciously living in any chosen soul, in any number of souls, all of them unconscious of their interchangeable burden" (pp. 204–205). Another instance of a character somewhat ambiguously "dying" and being resurrected in other guises occurs in *The Eye*: early in the story the narrator shoots himself but reappears, talking about himself in the third person, in refracted figures through the rest of the tale.

[1] V. Nabokov, *Poems* (New York: Doubleday and Co., Inc., 1959), p. 26.

Shade's comment on his own speculations about "resurrection" links dreams and the imagination with the afterlife:

> It isn't that we dream too wild a dream:
> The trouble is we do not make it seem
> Sufficiently unlikely; for the most
> We can think up is a domestic ghost. (P. 41.)

In Kinbote and his fantasy world of Zembla we have an imaginative "dream" which is both "sufficiently unlikely" and undomestic. Kinbote, the bearded, exotically attired pederast, is a complete contrast to the homely Frost-like poet who has been married for forty years to his high school sweetheart, just as the glittering world of Zembla is completely unlike the sleepy small town of New Wye.

Nabokov's description of a chess problem seems to me an appropriate analogue to the structural riddle and the mystification about the identities of the main characters in *Pale Fire*. To paraphrase the chess passage quoted in my introduction, *Pale Fire* is for the delectation of the expert reader. To the "inexpert" it might appear to be no more than a parody of literary criticism: a work consisting of a fine poem and a totally unrelated egocentric commentary, which reflects only the mad critic's fantasies. In this reading, Shade the poet and Kinbote the critic are two separate and contrasting identities. Kinbote is mad, and imagines that he is the exiled King Charles of Zembla. The "inexpert" solution to the meaning of the ending is that Shade, who looks like the vacationing Judge Goldsworth, is shot by an escaped lunatic who has been confined by the judge, although the mad Kinbote believes that the lunatic was an assassin from Zembla who intended to kill the exiled king. This solution provides us with the facile irony of having the distinguished poet die through a case of mistaken identity, just as his mad critic

destroys his lovely poem through misreading. Such a
course of events would render Shade's assertion that he
can create a "web of sense" completely absurd and ill-
founded, and the poet's striving for understanding and
pity would appear similarly futile. This is what Nabokov
would label "a fashionable avant-garde theme" which
even the "expert" reader might briefly entertain, and
which the author has carefully "planted" as well as
undermined.

꜔ But the re-reader will first of all notice certain pecu-
liarities about the names of the characters. The killer's
name is listed in the Index (p. 307) as "Gradus, alias
Jack Degree, de Grey, D'Argus, Vinogradus, Leningradus,
etc." "Gradus" in Latin means "step, *degree*." A *Gradus
ad Parnassum* is a dictionary used as an aid in writing
poetry, and literaly means "a step to the place where the
Muses live." "Shade" is defined by the dictionary as
"shadow, *degree* of darkness; a disembodied spirit; to un-
dergo and exhibit difference or variation." There is thus a
specific connection between Gradus and Shade, and the
suggestion that the two characters are aspects of a single
consciousness—that Gradus is a creation of the poet, a degree of Shade, or a step in the structure. Gradus, who is
repeatedly identified with the inevitable ending of the
poem—indeed, he arrives at the very last line—may be the
final tool used by the poet to complete his work and arrive
at Parnassus.[2]

[2] Kinbote describes Gradus' movement toward Shade: "The
force propelling him is the magic action of Shade's poem itself,
the very mechanism and sweep of verse, the powerful iambic mo-
tor" (p. 136). See also p. 78, where Gradus is made to exist entirely in terms of Shade's poetry, "breathing with the caesura." A
similar view of Gradus' role is expressed by Mary McCarthy in
her excellent article "Vladimir Nabokov's *Pale Fire*," *Encounter*,
XIX (1962), and in Carol T. Williams' " 'Web of Sense': *Pale Fire*
in the Nabokov Canon," *Critique*, VI (Winter, 1963).

The Latin word for "shade" is *opacitas*. The artist-protagonist of *Invitation to a Beheading*, in a political-literary trial, is repeatedly accused of "opacity," and he is the only "real" identity in a world of unreal, "translucent" souls.[3] This is Nabokov's image of the artist as a "solid" presence in a fictional world where all other objects are penetrated by his ray, though even the artist's "solidity" is illusory, an imaginative reflection of his actual self. This connotation of Shade's name is only one of numerous clues that he is the "real" author, returned from the "shades" of the literary underworld in order to exhibit variations or degrees of other characters.

Kinbote tells us that his name in Zemblan, "the tongue of the mirror" (p. 242), means "regicide" (p. 267). Kinbote's former, anagrammatic name is Botkin, which is listed in the Index as "king-bot"—for which read bot-fly, a parasitic larva in the cavities of various mammals including man. Sybil Shade refers to Kinbote as "a king-sized botfly; a macao worm; the monstrous parasite of a genius" (pp. 171–172). Thus Kinbote on the one hand is associated with Gradus, the regicide (Shade being the real king, who orders the novel), and on the other with his creator, Shade, whose "parasite" he is. If Gradus is a degree of Shade, an aid in completing the poem, and Kinbote is Shade's parasite, the "realistic" base of the "simple solution" consisting of poet, critic, and murderer begins to crumble. (In connection with the essential oneness of the three characters, it is useful to note that all three have the same birthday, July 5—though, appropriately, Shade is older than the other two. Both Kinbote and Gradus were born July 5, 1915, probably because Shade created them simultaneously.)

Further character amalgamations are suggested by Kin-

[3] *Invitation to a Beheading* (Greenwich, Conn.: Crest Books, 1960), esp. pp. 21–24.

bote's remark that "Hazel Shade resembled me in certain
respects" (p. 193), here mentioned in connection with
their interest in "twisted" mirror words. But in their un-
attractiveness, unpopularity, "difficult, morose" natures,
and inclinations toward the supernatural and toward
suicide, Kinbote and Hazel Shade are even more strikingly similar. We may recall V.'s description of Sebastian's process of artistic transference: Sebastian "had the
power to create simultaneously—and out of the very
things which distressed his mind—a fictitious and faintly
absurd character" (p. 114). It is possible that Shade's grief
at the suicide of his daughter might have translated itself
into the creation of the absurd yet suffering Kinbote.[4]

Another instance of a character from Shade's personal
life being mirrored in the commentary is Kinbote's recognition of the similarity between Sybil Shade, as depicted in the poem, and his own wife Disa, Duchess of
Great Payn and Mone (read "pain and moan"). Kinbote's
moving description of his "dream-love" for Disa parallels
Shade's feelings for his wife:

His dream-love for her exceeded in emotional tone, in spiritual passion and depth, anything he had experienced in his
surface existence. This love was like an endless wringing of
hands, like a blundering of the soul through an infinite maze
of hopelessness and remorse. They were, in a sense, amorous
dreams, for they were permeated with tenderness, with a longing to sink his head unto her lap and sob away the monstrous
past. . . . He absolutely had to find her at once to tell her
that he adored her, but the large audience before him separated him from the door, and the notes reaching him through
a succession of hands said that she was not available; that

[4] In the Index (p. 312), Hazel is defined as the "domestic ghost"
who "preferred the beauty of death to the ugliness of life," while
Kinbote is a character, according to Shade, "who deliberately peels
off a drab and unhappy past and replaces it with a brilliant
invention" (p. 238).

she was inaugurating a fire; that she had married an American businessman; that she had become a character in a novel; that she was dead. (Pp. 211–212.)

This passage is an intensified and tortured confession inspired by Shade's lines which themselves express passionate love. Shade's, however, is reciprocated and consummated:

> Come and be worshiped, come and be caressed,
> My dark Vanessa, crimson-barred, my blest
> My admirable butterfly! Explain
> How could you, in the gloom of Lilac Lane,
> Have let uncouth, hysterical John Shade
> Blubber your face, and ear, and shoulder blade?

> We have been married forty years. At least
> Four thousand times your pillow has been creased
> By our two heads. Four hundred thousand times
> The tall clock with the hoarse Westminster chimes
> Has marked our common hour. (Pp. 42–43.)

Kinbote's dream passion represents the hopeless, helpless, agonizing underside of Shade's more joyous and contented love. Kinbote's is the agony which lies beneath all love relationships: the sense of unworthiness, the gliding away of precious moments. Kinbote's inability to "find" Disa is an aspect of love's horror: the realization that the essence of the beloved is unattainable, the feeling that insurmountable obstacles prevent him from reaching her innermost soul.

All these "subliminal" connections between the poem and the commentary, between Shade's personal life and Kinbote's fictional existence, seem to me to invalidate the surface impression that the novel is about a mad critic's irrelevant comments on a lovely poem. The range of experience and emotion encompassed by *Pale Fire* comes from a single artistic sensibility dreaming an "unlikely" dream, and within the dream is his conscious emotional life (just as the poem exists within the commentary). In *Sebastian Knight*, V. finds it hard to believe that "the warmth, the tenderness, the beauty of [Sebastian's love for Clare] has not been gathered, and is not treasured somewhere, somehow, by some immortal witness of mortal life" (p. 87). It seems to be this fear of a personal vision dispersed, this need to preserve the sensations of one's consciousness, which motivate Nabokov's artist figures. He writes in *Speak, Memory* of "the utter degradation, ridicule, and horror of having developed an infinity of sensation and thought within a finite existence" (p. 226). The forays into artistic creation represent extensions of one's "finite existence." The "inviolable shade," the artwork, is not mortal.

But the artistic relationship can be looked at from several vantage points. The poet may be "immortal" in the sense that his consciousness outlives the immediate boundaries of each character he creates, but the fictional characters are "immortal" in a different way: they will continue to exist in the realm of literature long after the poet's finite sensibility has died. Thus, in one sense, the artistic creation bears "immortal witness" to the "mortal life" of its author, testifying to his having made an "imprint in the intimate texture of space." The dual application of the presence of an "immortal witness to mortal life" is constantly employed in *Pale Fire*. This process explains the idea behind the structure of the novel; it provides a connection between the poem and the commentary.

The reverse of this formula, the "immortality" of fictional characters who live in "the refuge of art," accounts for the fictional Kinbote's survival beyond Shade's dissolution. This idea seems to lurk behind various puzzling aspects of the novel, such as the seemingly obscure rele-

vance of the epigraph from Boswell's *Life of Johnson*:
"This reminds me of the ludicrous account he gave Mr.
Langton, of the despicable state of a young gentleman
of good family. 'Sir, when I heard of him last, he was
running about town shooting cats.' And then in a sort of
kindly reverie, he bethought himself of his own favorite
cat, and said, 'But Hodge shan't be shot: no, no, Hodge
shall not be shot.' " Shade tells us that he looks like Samuel Johnson (p. 267), and it is Shade who keeps Kinbote
from getting shot by Gradus. In Kinbote's recollection
of the murder scene, he feels Shade's hand pulling him
back "to the protection of his laurels." In his left hand
Kinbote holds in an envelope " 'the inviolable shade' "
(p. 294),[5] the poem itself. Thus Shade, the Samuel Johnson to Kinbote's Hodge, extends the "immortal refuge"
of his art ("his laurels") to his pet creation. I take the
epigraph to be another adumbration of the recurrent idea
in *Pale Fire* that the artist momentarily perishes with
each of his creations, in order to give life to a work of art.
The "inviolable shade" of the poem remains even when
the mortal Shade of the poet dies. And Shade can keep
Kinbote from getting shot and fading into oblivion by
immortalizing him in *Pale Fire*.

[5] Kinbote briefly identifies this quotation by adding: "to quote
Matthew Arnold, 1822–1888." More precisely, the phrase is from
"The Scholar Gypsy," line 212. Arnold's alienated exile, whose
chief interest is in learning from the gypsies the "arts to rule as
they desired / The workings of men's brains" (pp. 45–47), bears a
resemblance to Shade. The Scholar-Gypsy is driven, by his dual
identity, to abandon his staid, academic life and explore the wild,
uprooted existence of the gypsies. The context of line 212 suggests
many of Shade's themes: "Still nursing the unconquerable hope, /
Still clutching the inviolable shade, / With a free, onward impulse
brushing through" (lines 211–213). Shade's conclusion, after one
of the most dramatic revelations of fate and coincidence, is that
he can grope his way to some "faint hope" (p. 63). There is of
course in "the inviolable shade" a pun on the poet's name, and
the suggestion that he as artist will survive Gradus' attack.

The final summary of the entire plot of the novel also
suggests that Shade is "real" while the other characters
(Kinbote and Gradus) are fictional: "a lunatic who in-
tends to kill an imaginary king, another lunatic who
fancies himself to be that king, and a distinguished old
poet who stumbles by chance into the line of fire, and
perishes in the clash between the two figments" (p. 301).
The "clash between the two figments" is the plot of the
commentary, and if the lunatic (Gradus) and the imaginary king (Kinbote) are "figments," they are figments of
the omniscient author's imagination. The poet perishes
metaphorically, by giving himself up to the fictional clash,
by transposing his own personality into that of the figments. He merges into the less "realistic" elements of the
novel.

The first few lines of the poem present a similar idea
through an image of multiple reflection:

> I was the shadow of the waxwing slain
> By the false azure in the windowpane;
> I was the smudge of ashen fluff—and I
> Lived on, flew on, in the reflected sky. (P. 33.)

Mary McCarthy explains the above lines as the image
"of a bird that has flown against a window and smashed
itself."[6] But the image is not *of a bird*, but of the *poet as
a bird*. Furthermore, it is, significantly, an image of the
poet as the *shadow* of a bird ("I was the shadow of the
waxwing"). This refracted shadow is essential to the pattern of the novel, and recurs not only in other metaphoric

[6] McCarthy, p. 72. While I acknowledge the value of many of
her findings and speculations, I think that her view of the novel
as a "shadow box" with false bottoms makes the pattern of the
relationship between the "real" Shade and the "fictional" Kinbote
unintelligible. She translates her explications into a series of successive planes of meaning, and thereby makes the novel into a
depressing semblance of coy clues for their own sake, an arch
regression leading nowhere.

images but also in the poet's identity in relation to his lunatic and his imaginary king. After Shade is shot, Kinbote describes him as lying "with open dead eyes directed up at the sunny evening azure" (p. 295), and the Index, under "Waxwing," lists "Bombycilla shadei" and remarks: "interesting association belatedly realized" (p. 315). The "belated" realization is probably that of the reader, who is here explicitly shown the connection between the figure of Shade and Gradus, the shadow of the waxwing. Gradus, who tails the movement of the poem, kills Shade—or ends the poem—but he is finally only an insubstantial adjunct of his supposed victim.

Pnin, during his first heart attack, sees the design on the wallpaper coming to life. This is compared to "the reflection of an inside object in a windowpane with the outside scenery perceived through the same glass" (*Pnin*, p. 24). The windowpane is the borderline between the artist and his creation, the medium of the artistic imagination. In terms of the total structure of *Pale Fire*, the "inside object" is the poem, the "outside scenery" is the commentary, especially the Zemblan landscape. The "windowpane" which reflects both the poem and the commentary is the poet's imagination. (The "shadow of the waxwing," the creative impulse, smashes itself against the "windowpane" of the imagination, and it is transformed, "slain.") The artistic process of transformation does not end in death, but in the birth of another object: "I was the smudge of ashen fluff—and I / Lived on, flew on, in the reflected sky." The "reflected sky" is the realm of art, which provides its own kind of life; the "slain" waxwing is translated from physical reality to imaginative reality.

The initial mirroring process is reflected vision. The first concave mirror is the poet's eye, which transmits perceived objects to a timeless, "nether" reality:

> Whatever in my field of vision dwelt—
> An indoor scene, hickory leaves, the svelte
> Stilettos of a frozen stillicide—
> Was printed on my eyelids' nether side
> Where it would tarry for an hour or two,
> And while this lasted all I had to do
> Was close my eyes to reproduce the leaves,
> Or indoor scene, or trophies of the eaves. (P. 34.)

Kinbote's dictionary defines "stillicide" as " 'a succession of drops falling from the eaves, eavesdrop, cavesdrop.' " And his comment on the lines is: "The bright frost has eternalized the bright eavesdrop" (p. 79). Shade is of course referring to his seeing "dagger-shaped" frozen drops extending from the lower roof ("eaves") of the house. A "still" can also be a "single photographic picture of an object." In the beginning of the stanza, Shade described the first step in the poetic process as the "eyes" taking "photographs." These "still" photographs are then stored on the "nether side" of the poet's vision, and instead of the original "single picture" they become a multiple and inverse reflection. Stillicide is the falling drop transfixed by the eye and made timeless by memory. Hence, artistic creation is literally a "stillicide" (false etymology but correct pun), a "slaying" of the single image and the substitution of a refracted one.

This idea echoes and further clarifies the opening metaphor. As the poet's self is reflected in the "windowpane" of his imagination, the iron ring of his close-fitting single personality is transformed into a series of receding images of other selves, Kinbote and Gradus. It is appropriate that the word "stillicide" should remind Kinbote of Gradus, who appears here as "the shadow of regicide" (p. 79). Shade's slaying by Gradus is no more than a "stillicide," a melodic fall, the poet's conscious decision to kill his own single self, and to "live on, fly on," as Gradus and Kinbote. Kinbote's statement about "the

bright frost" and "the bright eavesdrop" is a punning
clue to the single authorship of Shade. Shade is repeatedly
compared to Robert Frost in *Pale Fire*, and Kinbote is a
persistent eavesdropper and peeping Tom. Thus the sentence "the bright frost has eternalized the bright eavesdrop" could mean: "Shade has immortalized Kinbote."

The variant for Shade's lines 39–40 is listed as: "and
home would haste my thieves, / The sun with stolen ice,
the moon with leaves" (p. 79). If we compare the final
lines with the variants, we find that "eyes" has been substituted for "thieves." Thus the poet's eyes "thieve" objects from nature. The variant lines remind Kinbote of a
passage from *Timon of Athens* (IV. iii), but he gives us
only a rough retranslation from the Zemblan version of
the English original. The reader who looks up the reference in *Timon* is rewarded with the source for the novel's
title, as noted by Mary McCarthy (Carol T. Williams adds
to this source a reference in *Hamlet* I.5.90):

> The sun's a thief, and with his great attraction
> Robs the vast sea. The moon's an arrant thief,
> And her pale fire she snatches from the sun.
> The sea's a thief, whose liquid surge resolves
> The moon into salt tears. (*Timon*, IV.iii.439–443.)

This image of cosmic thievery seems to be a projection of
the natural world in terms of reflections. The artist sees
the world as a vast artwork, where objects exist only subjectively, in terms of mirrorings. Shade describes the
natural phenomena which surround him as "painted
parchment papering our cage" (p. 36), the "cage" being
our finite existence. "Pale fire" is the glow of the imaginative vision on the eyelid's "nether side," the reflection
shadowed on the "windowpane" of the imagination, the
fragmentation of a "still" photograph, the end-product
of a vast process of transformation or thievery. As the
hero remarks near the end of *The Gift*, when the coinci-

dental patterns of the plot are bared: "The most enchant-
ing things in nature and art are based on deception" (p.
376). The art metaphor applied to the quotation from
Shakespeare casts the poet as "the sun," whose rays of
light are reflected by the mirror of the sea. The moon, the
artwork, by looking into the same mirror, picks up the
reflected rays of the sun. The sea, the "windowpane" on
which both the "inside object" and the "outside scenery"
(the poet and his creation) meet, distills ("resolves") the
impact of the artwork into emotion ("salt tears").

Emotion validates the "reality" of the reflection in the
windowpane. Poetic significance for Nabokov is compounded of widening circles of personal discoveries leading to illusory patterns which nevertheless produce "real"
sensations of brightness and beauty. There are also receding circles of imaginative control within *Pale Fire*: the
existence of an omniscient author is glimpsed by Shade
when he muses in his poem about the pleasures of perceiving in his *life* certain events which appear to be "coincidences," but which on another level are games played
by "them":

> It did not matter who they were. No sound,
> No furtive light came from their involute
> Abode, but there they were, aloof and mute,
> Playing a game of worlds, promoting pawns
> To ivory unicorns and ebon fauns; . . . (P. 63.)

The thinning fictional surface here points to the controlling hand of the author as the God of his characters. But
Shade, though he recognizes the limitations on his freedom, can duplicate both the process and the consequent
emotional satisfaction of imaginative creation. In remem-
bering his life with his wife and daughter, Shade fixes
and formalizes the design of their evenings as "a tryptich
or a three-act play / In which portrayed events forever
stay" (p. 46). Recollected and rearranged, the figures and

emotions of the poet's personal life crystallize and become permanent through artifice. The tryptich of Shade,
Kinbote, and Gradus also forms a tripartite structure in
the shifting geography of New Wye, Zembla, and the
mirror world of the reality of the novel, further triplicated
in the successive levels of poem, commentary, and index.

Shade's attempt to understand and assimilate the game
in which he is a pawn is repeated through Kinbote's ma-
neuvers in trying to place himself and his fantasies into
the poem by constructing a commentary. As Shade is a
pawn of the celestial players' web, so Kinbote is a pawn
of Shade's design, and both characters merge into the
author of the Notes. Shade and Kinbote project their
private feelings and obsessions through literary forms:
the autobiographic poem and the autobiographic commentary. But Shade achieves an awareness of artistic
methods of perception which remains closed to Kinbote.
Shade's revelation proceeds from the deception of a "mis-
print" to an illumination of the "web of sense" which he
himself can create through art:

> But all at once it dawned on me that *this*
> Was the real point, the contrapuntal theme;
> Just this: not text, but texture; not the dream
> But topsy-turvical coincidence,
> Not flimsy nonsense, but a web of sense.
> Yes! It sufficed that I in life could find
> Some kind of link-and-bobolink, some kind
> Of correlated pattern in the game,
> Plexed artistry, and something of the same
> Pleasure in it as they who played it found. (P. 63.)

The "contrapuntal theme" of *Pale Fire* manifests itself
in the novel's concern with the other side of conscious
existence. In the first part—the poem—this concern is
explicitly expressed in the speculations about death and
the hereafter. In the commentary, we find the "contrapuntal" concern—a variation on the same basic theme—

in the exploration of the unconscious aspect of the imagination as embodied by Kinbote. The "correlated patterns" in the novel are placed as clues to its meaning: for
instance, Shade's first death-like trance occurs in boyhood
while watching a "tin wheelbarrow pushed by a tin boy"
(p. 38), a toy which Kinbote sees in Shade's basement.
("The boy was a little Negro of painted tin with a key-
hole in his side and no breadth to speak of, just consisting
of two more or less fluid profiles.") Shade tells Kinbote
that the boy in the wheelbarrow is a kind of *memento
mori* (p. 137). In another context Kinbote recalls his
"young Negro gardener" (p. 217), and at the end of the
poem, Shade is watching this gardener pushing a wheelbarrow. This is when Gradus, the death of the poem,
overtakes him. The pattern is thus deliberate, and the
death preordained by symmetrical artistry. It is very
possible—since each of his death-like trances transports
Shade to strange lands and sights—that the Zembla story,
which follows the second appearance of the Negro boy
and the wheelbarrow, is a dream which occurs during
the trance, combining some facts of Shade's everyday
life, and using the Ur-figure of his colleague Botkin. The
suspended poetic imagination invests Botkin with the
(literally) "unconscious" fantasies of the poet. Or, the
gardener-wheelbarrow recurrence could be the imprint
of the author of which Shade is unaware.

The symptoms of Shade's "swoon" at the age of eleven
are described successively as "a sudden sunburst" and
"black night." The result is a feeling of ubiquitousness:
"That blackness was sublime. / I felt distributed through
space and time" (p. 38). This sensation is the equivalent
of authorial omniscience, and foreshadows Shade's ability
to transform and nearly obliterate his ordinary surroundings—an ability manifested in the commentary. The later
attack after his lecture produces an unearthly vision:

> I can't tell you how
> I knew—but I did know that I had crossed
> The border. Everything I loved was lost
> But no aorta could report regret.
> A sun of rubber was convulsed and set;
> And blood-black nothingness began to spin
> A system of cells interlinked within
> Cells interlinked within cells interlinked
> Within one stem. And dreadfully distinct
> Against the dark, a tall white fountain played.
> I realized, of course, that it was made
> Not of our atoms; that the sense behind
> The scene was not our sense. (p. 59.)

The sun and blackness are present in both seizures, but the startling image of the fountain inspires more awe than elation. It may be that the sunlight is an emblem of nearly blinding illumination, and that the fountain is related to the Romantic metaphor of the mind and the creative faculty. (There may be a specific allusion to the most famous of Romantic dream-fountains, the one in "Kubla Khan.")

Through its numerous allusions to Romantic poetry (in addition to neo-classical sources), *Pale Fire* alerts us to its interest in the Romantic sensibility achieved through the combined figures of its death-obsessed poet and despairingly religious madman. This influence may also account for the teasing unfinished form of the poem (and suggests that Kinbote's assurance that the thousandth line was intended to be the same as the first may be deliberately planted misinformation). Underneath the careful patterning of the poem lurks an awareness of chaos, insoluble mysteries, and irrational hopes and agonies. These undercurrents are openly exploited in the commentary, but their presence in the poem is usually overlooked.[7] Shade's recurrent concern with the "hereafter" (p. 41)

---

[7] Field states matter-of-factly that "the poem itself, after all, is hardly 'abstruse' " (p. 308).

or the "inadmissible abyss" (p. 39) is partly the quest for
the source which shapes the form of events in life, partly
the nature of poetic inspiration and of the mind. Poetic
inspiration and the pattern of beauty, as in Wordsworth,
are sometimes explicitly located outside man (p. 63),
sometimes within the ability of the imagination to shape
a world of its own, and sometimes seen as simultaneously
manifested in external nature and paralleled through artistic creation. Some of these Romantic sentiments are
expressed in Wordsworth's "Ode to Lycoris":

> But something whispers to my heart
> That as we downward tend,
> Lycoris! life requires an *art*
> To which our souls must bend;
> A skill—to balance and supply;
> And, ere the flowing fount be dry,
> As soon it must, a sense to sip,
> Or drink, with no fastidious lip.
>   (III, 37–44, italics in original.)

Wordsworth's ode emphasizes the conjunction of soul
and art—the former apprenticed to the craft of the latter.
It also employs the image of the "fount" as the source of
the creative power. It seems to me that Shade's treasured
remembrance of the vision of the fountain deliberately
alludes to Wordsworth:

> Often when troubled by the outer glare
> Of street and strife, inward I'd turn, and there,
> There in the background of my soul it stood,
> Old Faithful! And its presence always would
> Console me wonderfully, (p. 60.)

This is not only a probable specific echo of "I Wandered
Lonely as a Cloud" ("For oft when on my couch I lie . . ."),
but generally suggests the Wordsworthian recollection as
something intact, sustaining, inwardly preserved amidst
later surroundings. Shade finally turns from seeking a

"twin display" of his fountain in its naked form (pp. 60–62) and translates his otherworldly trance (the mysterious source of the imagination) into individually colored experiences found "in life" which reproduce the "pleasure" (p. 63), if not the form, of his awesome vision. The discovery of this possibility of "texture," "coincidence," "web of sense," "link-and-bobolink," "correlated pattern," and its concomitant Romantic expressive theory of art (the "pleasure" deriving from this discovery is both generated *by* and *for* the poet), is not only a turning point in the poem—and hence in Shade's consciousness—but serves as a hint of the formal aesthetic principle connecting the poem and the commentary.

Shade's perception that he can create "texture" and a "web of sense" through "plexed artistry," and that he can find "pleasure" in the "game," is mirrored in Kinbote's understanding of the impact of art. But, characteristically, Kinbote's findings express the intense vision of a tormented soul:

I do not consider myself a true artist save in one matter: I can do what only a true artist can do—pounce upon the forgotten butterfly of revelation, wean myself abruptly from the habit of things, see the warp and the weft of that web. Solemnly I weighed in my hand what I was carrying under my left armpit, and for a moment I found myself enriched with indescribable amazement as if informed that fireflies were making decodable signals on behalf of stranded spirits, or that a bat was writing a legible tale of torture in the bruised and branded sky. (P. 289.)

The "contrapuntal" treatment of a revelation of artistic meaning is provided by these two passages: one from the poem, the other from the commentary. As in the dual presentation of love (of Sybil and Disa), we are given the underside of ordered and regulated pattern, literally the "warp and the weft of that web." What Kinbote is carrying under his left armpit is the envelope containing Shade's poem, *Pale Fire*. The revelation thus symbolically emanates from the poem, the "web of sense" of the entire novel. But the "warp and the weft," the "tale of torture" and the possible comic distortion of that "sense," are in the commentary. The poem, the finished artwork, is surrounded by the fantasies, dreams, parodies, "blind throbbings," and variants which attend its composition.

Like Kinbote's conclusion of the discussion on methods of painting, the correlated fabrication of poem and commentary demonstrates Nabokov's dictum that " 'reality' is neither the subject nor the object of true art, which creates its own special reality" (p. 130). And the special "reality" of *Pale Fire*, the relationship between more and less "realistic" creations, is so delicately, brilliantly, and humorously woven that the effect of the whole is the reader's great pleasure in "plexed artistry."

Kinbote is a patchwork creation containing Botkin the Russian scholar, Kinbote the mad Zemblan exile (alias King Charles), and, above all, an element of Shade's "special rich streak of magical madness" (p. 296) which is missing from the poem's "web of sense." Kinbote, as madman, is a translucent figment penetrated by the rays of a more solid character. This translucence is affirmed both in Kinbote's discussion on madness and by the ending of the commentary. Kinbote tells us that Zemblan theologians believe "that even the most demented mind still contains within its diseased mass a sane basic particle that survives death and suddenly expands, bursts out as it were, in peals of healthy and triumphant laughter when the world of timorous fools and trim blockheads has fallen away far behind" (p. 237). "The sane basic particle that survives death" is the author beneath his mad creation. The "peals of healthy and triumphant laughter" occur later, on the last page of the commentary, when the voice of Kinbote, described as "plated" with the poetry of Shade, "bullet-proof" against mortality, complains that his "notes and self are petering out." But, as the terminology suggests, this too is only a metaphorical "dying." The character of Kinbote will be transmuted into "other forms" by the imagination: "I shall continue to exist. I may assume other disguises, other forms, but I shall try to exist." For the moment, however, Kinbote dissolves into a shade of Nabokov: "I may turn up yet, on another campus, as an old, happy, healthy, heterosexual Russian, a writer in exile, sans fame, sans future, sans audience, sans anything but his art" (p. 301).

Kinbote feels complacently assured that without his notes "Shade's text simply has no human reality at all, since the human reality of such a poem as his . . . has to depend entirely on the reality of its author and his surroundings, attachments, and so forth, a reality that only my notes can provide" (pp. 28–29). This statement, which on one level parodies critical attitudes toward literature, also contains a serious clue to the meaning of the novel. Kinbote's notes tell us practically nothing of Shade's everyday surroundings, but they present the fantasy world of Zembla in great detail. But this fantasy world is, in an important sense, part of Shade's "reality"—the reality of his imagination. And the notes *do* provide this imaginative context of a fantasy world which is a dimension of the poem, but is not included in it. I am not suggesting, as Stegner does, that the commentary is more "imaginative" than the poem, or that the novel culminates in the supposed joke "that Kinbote, crazy as he may be, has actually *understood* Shade's poem, and has structured in his fantastic commentary a story that mirrors Shade's notion of symmetrical fate." The supposition of such an "understanding" on Kinbote's part would make it necessary for him to have an autonomous identity that

outlives and outshines Shade's. In keeping with this interpretation, Stegner maintains that the poem is a "fabrication of the artist-madman Kinbote." It is then no wonder
that Stegner dislikes *Pale Fire*; given his reading, the
novel would indeed be a "joke," a vast inversion and
critical parody, pointing to nothing but that madmen can
write sane poems.[8]

Even Andrew Field, in an otherwise excellent analysis
of the connection between Nabokov's unfinished *Solus
Rex* and *Pale Fire*, finds the commentary more interesting
than the poem: "The real irony of the title *Pale Fire* is
that, fine as Shade's poem is, it is pale beside the mad and
wonderful work of art and distortion that whirls der-
vishly around it—just as the artist's life must pale before his art." I suppose that the relative "paleness" of
poem to commentary is a delicate matter of preference,
but Field seems to be forced into the value judgment he
makes because he wants to fit his theory about "the
artist's life" versus "his art" into *Pale Fire*. He elaborates
this theory by suggesting that this novel is emblematic of
a general phenomenon: "Flaubert is not nearly "as large"
as Emma Bovary, . . . and even the giant Tolstoy is small
beside his Anna Karenina. This, in art, is an elemental
truth: as the work comes closer and closer to true great-
ness, the protagonist and the novel as a whole must chal-
lenge and finally eclipse, in varying degrees, the creator."[9]

Pale Fire seems to me to be clearly about the artist and
his creation. But I do not see how Shade's poem, which is
itself an artifact, can be equated with the "real" life or
self of the artist, which is then "eclipsed" by his "work."
The poem, after all, is not Shade's "real" life or self, but
an imaginative reconstruction and rearrangement. The
poem and the commentary are both "works" by a con-

[8] Stegner, pp. 128, 130.
[9] Field, pp, 308, 316.

trolling author, each representing a different aspect of his imaginative reality. I feel that the novel does not force us to choose between the poem and the commentary. In their different ways, each artwork is interesting and beautiful. *Pale Fire* explores the multiple, terrifyingly rich personality of the artist, and celebrates his capacity to create two works of art utterly different in genre, form, and tone, at the same time related in subject. The poem, which might represent Shade's contemplative and emotional life, uses the materials of the poet's "real" life as recognizable springboards. The commentary fictionally develops the poet's fantasies, fears, and loneliness, through the guise of portraying a mad pervert and placing this fictional pervert in the imagined reality of the poet's small-town life.[10] But the "realistic" base of the novel is a kind of cage, outside which the omniscient author, not quite refined out of existence, fits the poetic and prosaic elements into the theme of fate and death.

Is there an "irony," as Field claims, in the title *Pale Fire*, which would suggest that the poem "pales" before the commentary? The phrase "pale fire" occurs in the

[10] This doubling of personality and the process of imaginary mirroring is suggested in Marvell's "The Garden":

> The mind, that ocean where each kind
> Does straight its own resemblance find;
> Yet it creates transcending these,
> Far other worlds and other seas,
> Annihilating all that's made
> To a green thought in a green shade. (Lines 43–48.)

Sybil is a translator of Marvell and Donne into French, though this particular poem is not explicitly mentioned in the text. (In *Ada*, however, Nabokov makes central use of "The Garden.") The reference to the theory that the mind, like the ocean, contains the double of everything in "reality," the extension of mere doubling into the creation of "far other worlds and seas," and the "green shade" of the poet may be coincidental mirrorings between Marvell and Nabokov.

Foreword, when Kinbote sees Shade burning his rejected
first drafts like a "mourner" at the "pale fire of the incinerator" (p. 15). The glow of the incinerator, like the
moonshine in *Timon*, may refer to the creative fire which
prunes and purifies the initial conception into the final
work of art. It is probably a mistake to interpret "pale" in
the pejorative sense of weakness or diminished intensity.
Rather, the novel seems to contrast the "sunburst" and
the "sun of rubber" of Shade's otherworldly trances with
the "pale fire" of a shimmering, opaque light which is the
product of deliberate artistic technique. After all, *Pale
Fire* is the title not only of the poem, but of the entire
novel. Poem and commentary are both irradiated by the
moonshine of the author's imagination; they do not represent "life" versus "art," but each reflects a different
aspect of the artist's psychology, and different techniques
of artistry.

The imaginative context of the poem further prevents
its being reduced to signify simply the "life" of the artist.
The poem often reflects back upon itself: a work of art
reminding the reader that it is contained within a work of
art. One of the most teasing instances of this self-
reflection occurs in the penultimate stanza:

> I feel I understand
> Existence, or at least a minute part
> Of my existence, only through my art,
> In terms of combinational delight;
> And if my private universe scans right,
> So does the verse of galaxies divine
> Which I suspect is an iambic line.
>
> . . . .
>
> So this alarm clock let me set myself,
> Yawn, and put back Shade's "Poems" on their shelf. (p. 69).

The seemingly prosaic details of Shade's life have all been
given a "combinational," "iambic" pattern. The last line
suggests that everything we have been reading so far has

been a poem out of a volume of Shade's "Poems," and this added perspective of regression reinforces the sense of a rarefied artistic "reality" radiating from the poem. Kinbote tells us that the first and the last lines of the poem were intended to be identical. The first line is "I was the shadow of the waxwing slain," which is a statement about the relationship of the artist and the process of fictional transformation. But perhaps Shade intended to let the poem stand as it is. At any rate, Nabokov has obviously allowed the "incompleteness." Shade tells Kinbote that he is finished except for "a few trifles" (p. 288), and within the poem he muses on this aphorism: "Man's life as commentary to abstruse / Unfinished poem. Note for further use" (p. 67).

As the poem now stands, it ends with the vision of the gardener with the wheelbarrow, the symbolic pattern woven by the author to indicate that the poet will now "die," as he has done several times within the poem. In this way the poem is not closed off from the commentary by means of a circular pattern, but rather flows into the commentary in a spiral form which is Nabokov's favorite image of timelessness and artistic continuity.

Much confusion about which figure is the "primary author," and which artwork is a "gloss" to the other, would be avoided if the reader were to remind himself of the fact that the poem is completely self-contained and self-explanatory, while the commentary, as it stands, does not make sense without the poem. The poem can be read alone; the commentary cannot. Starting from this simple observation, the idea that the poem is a "gloss" to the commentary is immediately refuted. But, as I have tried to show, there are multiple cross-references and images in the commentary which "light up" some of the "under-sides" of the poem. The two artworks are meaningfully juxtaposed; although the poem is self-contained, it is nevertheless open to extension, elaboration, and inverse reflections. The poet's "death" at the end of the poem is a "deception," an illusion produced by the termination of one artwork. But this "deception" lends a "reality" to the other artwork, since Shade's imagination creates the continuation to the poem, the commentary.

The novel starts with the words *Pale Fire*, referring to the poem; the commentary ends with Gradus, the step to Parnassus; and the Index last lists "Zembla," which is Parnassus itself, the land of semblance, of art. The experience of the novel has taken us from the poem to the realm of poetic imagination. Both of these are contained in the mind of the artist. The poem presents Shade's obsession with the "abyss" of death and the hereafter. The commentary is the fantasy exploration of that abyss through the process of artistic creation. The pattern of *Pale Fire*—a novel about the search for and finding of psychological and metaphysical patterns—is the transformation and enrichment of different levels of the artistic imagination. Its form is the interwoven web of poem and commentary. Its meaning is the texture and impression of beauty resulting from the conjunction.

IV

LOLITA
The
Quest for Ecstasy

THE FORM and movement of *Lolita* are shaped by a dual task: to record the emotional apotheosis of the narrator's passion for a nymphet, and to transform his story into a work of art which will immortalize that passion. Thus the question of the nature of artistic creation is posed directly by the witty pedant, obsessive pervert, and ecstatic lover whose personality and motivation constitute one of the implicit themes of his memoir. Humbert Humbert is constantly conscious of the difficulties of creating a vehicle adequate to his adored subject and to his purpose of explaining, justifying, and condemning his role in Lolita's life.

Although the novel is a memoir narrated in the first person, there are themes and revelations of which Humbert is not fully in control. The striking verisimilitude which Nabokov creates through the mask of Humbert is only one aspect of a shifting tale. Despite the sharpness

of observation, the flawless ear for dialogue, the detailed
evocation of everyday American scenes, Humbert attempts to manipulate his readers; and he is manipulated,
in turn, without being aware of it. Critics have posed the
question: "Is there a voice behind Humbert?" and have
answered in the negative. But "point of view" need not
be expressed through a separate voice; in Nabokov's case
it is more a network of details behind and around Humbert which is not of his conscious making, and of which
he may be unaware. After all, Aubrey McFate, the dramatization of destiny as decreed by the omniscient author, is not Humbert's agent; and Humbert himself, when
Lolita reveals the name of her abductor, bows to a larger
fictional necessity.

In significant and easily recognizable ways *Lolita* is
rooted in a realistic convention, a lifelike density which
is one of its most pleasurable achievements. Humbert,
too, has a certain consistency of tone and characterization: he does not fade into the papier-mâché backdrop,
nor does he "peter out" to merge and disappear into his
creator, as do most other Nabokovian main characters.
The following remarks about the theme of art as suggested by and glimpsed through the narrative do not
mean to deny the compelling presence of the realistic
foreground, but point to an aspect of the novel wherein
many of Humbert's aims and pronouncements converge
with his desires.

As my analyses of *Sebastian Knight* and *Pale Fire* have
demonstrated, the theme of artistic creation runs through
all of Nabokov's works, sometimes treated seriously,
sometimes through parody. He enjoys combining the
earnest declaration with its tongue-in-cheek counterpart;
the true ecstasy with its mawkish replica. The intricate
structure of *Lolita* comprises a number of themes and
metaphors, all of which are fitted into the quasi-realistic

American setting and yet extend the implications of Humbert's passion for nymphets into a treatment of the thrills of a butterfly hunt, the problems of a chess game, and assorted parodies of traditional and contemporary topics.[1] Nevertheless, the theme of artistic creation deserves particular attention: an illuminating and pervasive motif throughout the book, it is reflected in the "moral apotheosis" of H.H., the role of Lolita, and the form of the entire novel. In view of a certain aspect of Nabokov's definition of fiction and art (as the realm where the norm is "ecstasy"), Humbert's obsession is best described as "artistic." The emotional intensity, coupled with the stylistic care which Humbert lavishes on his Lolita (and Nabokov on his *Lolita*), strives to attain a beauty and perfection which is closest to "aesthetic bliss."

In most of Nabokov's novels, the private vision of love creates a world of significance and value for the lover. The narrator of "Spring in Fialta," happily married, admits his "hopeless" love for another woman and thus understands "why a piece of tinfoil had sparkled so on the pavement, why the gleam of a glass had trembled on a tablecloth, why the sea was ashimmer: somehow, by im-

[1] For a general summary of "clues and allusions" see C. R. Proffer, *Keys to Lolita* (Bloomington: Indiana University Press, 1968); also see Diana Butler on the butterfly theme ("Lolita Lepidoptera," *New World Writing* No. 16 [Philadelphia and New York, 1960], pp. 58–84); Lionel Trilling on the troubadour theme ("The Last Lover: V.N.'s *Lolita*," *Encounter*, XI, No. 4 [1958], 9–19); Conrad Brenner on the "perversion" of conventional subjects in Nabokov's works ("Nabokov: The Art of the Perverse," *New Republic*, June 23, 1958, pp. 18–21); G. D. Josipovici on parody as a means of turning words into emotion ("Lolita: Parody and the Pursuit of Beauty," *Critical Quarterly*, VI [1964], 35–48); and A. E. DuBois on "Poe and *Lolita*" *College English Assn. Critic*, XXVI, No. 6 [1964], 1, 7), which is an article worthy of Kinbote himself, and ends with this statement: "I somehow feel insulted. But certainly *Lolita* should be added to the bibliography of reflections about Poe."

perceptible degrees, the white sky above Fialta had got
saturated with sunshine, and now it was sun-pervaded
throughout, and this brimming white radiance grew
broader and broader. . . ."[2] The illumination of the interior consciousness comes with the feeling for another
being which results in a painful understanding of one's
own isolation. The lover's passion is rarely reciprocated,
nor is he allowed to rest in the joy of possessing his
beloved.[3]

Many of Nabokov's minor artists enact a search for
the meaning of the relationship between fate and passion.
The torment and elusiveness of this search is frequently
represented through the symptoms of perversion and
madness. But each artist-hero constructs private designs
or quirky games which alleviate and approximate the
anxieties and joys of his emotional life. Through his
characters' absorption in a personal cult, Nabokov expresses the uniqueness of every personality.

Most of the time the hero is forced to rest in the torture
of disunity, prey to the tricks of others as well as his
own weaknesses. Yet there is a recurring element of
beatitude in his torture. The Nabokovian lover relishes
the twofold nature of reality, in which the vulgarly obvious and everyday object has a profundity and fineness

---

[2] "Spring in Fialta," in *Nabokov's Dozen* (Garden City: Doubleday and Co., 1958), p. 38.

[3] At the moment that he confesses his passion, Nina's response
reflects the impossibility of communion: " 'Look here—what if I
love you?' Nina glanced at me, I repeated those words, I wanted
to add . . . but something like a bat passed swiftly across her face,
a quick, queer, almost ugly expression, and she, who would utter
coarse words with perfect simplicity, became embarrassed; I also
felt awkward. . . . 'Never mind, I was only joking,' I hastened to
say, lightly encircling her waist" (pp. 37–38). The nostalgia and
tenderness which the narrator offers is rejected for mysterious
reasons—perhaps because the burden of love is too painful or too
demanding.

available to him alone. His point of view is determined
by the "reality" of his desire. Thus Lolita's conventionality throws Humbert's ideal view of her into sharper
and more poignant relief, making his fantasy-vision all
the more precious by its precariousness. Lolita's shortcomings as a human being parallel the shortcomings of
the literary form which depicts her. She has the same
relation to the original Annabel of Humbert's youth as
the finished novel has to its initial conception. Humbert
describes his love for Annabel as a state where "the
spiritual and the physical had been blended in us with
a perfection that must remain incomprehensible to the
matter-of-fact, crude, standard-brained youngsters of
today" (p. 16). The fact that Lolita is presented largely
as such a "youngster," and yet eclipses the sensitive
sea-nymphet for Humbert, suggests that the imagination
both relishes and transcends the physical world. The
material for the imagination may lie in the physical
world. But the product of the imagination is transformed
into a passionately emotional object, which then lives
independent of any conventional "reality." What H.H.
overlooks until it is too late is the unique mystery in
even such seemingly conventional characters as his
nymphet.

In his *Nikolai Gogol,* Nabokov praises *The Government Inspector* (which he calls *The Government Specter*)
for "blending in a special way different aspects of vulgarity so that the prodigious artistic merit of the final
result is due (as with all masterpieces) not to what is
said but to how it is said."[4] Similarly, Nabokov finds
that in *The Overcoat,* "the real plot . . . lies in the style,
in the inner structure of this transcendental anecdote."[5]

[4] V. Nabokov, *Nikolai Gogol* (New York: New Directions, 1959),
p. 56.
[5] *Ibid.,* p. 144.

So too in Nabokov's works, the narrator is often deliberately placed in conventional situations from a Bildungsroman, a sentimental novel, or a mystery story.
Instead of minimizing the traditional nature of such passages, Nabokov describes these scenes in exaggerated
and self-conscious style.

Much of Humbert's imaginative creation is chronicled
through such stylistic devices. His rival is repeatedly pic-
tured as a "well-known" author, a purveyor of banalities
and sham artistry: an exploiter of public shallowness,
ignorance, and bad taste. The rival is sometimes the
hero's clever, despised alter ego. He stages the conventional scenes in order to torment the hero, or to seduce
the tantalizing, elusive woman who embodies both the
emotional and artistic hopes of the protagonist. This
theme is used also in Nabokov's early novel, *Laughter
in the Dark*.[6] The woman may be vulgar, mediocre, or
shallow; but as Diana Butler notes in her persuasive
essay on the butterfly theme in *Lolita*: "Nabokov tells
us that the object of passion is unimportant, but that the
nature of passion is constant."[7]

At the same time, the self-mocking commentary of the
narrators on their own passionate involvements, the self-
conscious dissection by the author of his own work, and
the shifting nature of the characters within each work
suggest that there is no stable, empirical "reality" in
which the object of passion and the lover can meet.
Nabokov's way of constantly reworking and varying the
theme of artistic creation reflects his belief that "verisi-

[6] The hated rival of "Spring in Fialta" is described as someone
who has "mastered the art of verbal invention to perfection," but
has no "heart," just as Axel Rex of *Laughter in the Dark* is a
caricaturist who enjoys only the distorted images of his own
twisted imagination.

[7] Butler, p. 75.

militude" exists only in relation to imaginative landscapes, and that the final and unique "truth" about a novel lies in the artist's self-contained fictional construct. This attitude toward "reality" as something which is entirely controlled and fashioned by the author is an essential explanation of much of the mystification, maddening inconstancy, and continual character shifts which are so typical of Nabokov's novels. In answer to an interviewer's question about whether his characters ever "take hold" of him, Nabokov replied: "I have never experienced this. . . . I am the perfect dictator in that private world, insofar as I alone am responsible for its stability and truth."[8]

The emphatically "private" nature of Nabokov's view of art and reality is paralleled in the novels by the jealously guarded unique obsession of many of the characters. The uniqueness of *Lolita*, of course, lies partly in its being a love story in which a vulgar, unromantic twelve-year-old is the object of passion, while her mother, full-blown and conventionally seductive, is viewed with distaste. While the theme of an affair between the lodger and the mother is an obvious cliché, the agonizing love for a slangy twelve-year-old is a delectable taboo. Throughout *Lolita* there is persistent identification between Humbert as lover and Humbert as artist, between the everyday, sentimental-novel existence of Lolita, and her mysterious Humbertian transformation: "Neither is she the fragile child of a feminine novel. What drives me insane is the twofold nature of this nymphet, . . . this mixture in my Lolita of tender dreamy childishness and a kind of eerie vulgarity, stemming from the snub-nosed cuteness of ads and magazine pictures . . . ; all this gets mixed up with the exquisite stainless tenderness seeping through

[8] Appel, "An Interview with Vladimir Nabokov," p. 133.

the musk and the mud, through the dirt and the death, oh God, oh God! And what is most singular is that she, *this* Lolita, *my* Lolita, has individualized the writer's ancient lust, so that above and over everything there is— Lolita" (p. 43). Humbert later characterizes his writings as "nightmare curlicues . . . ; hideous hieroglyphics . . . of my fatal lust" (p. 46), and his first orgasm of vicarious pleasure is described as being "suspended on the brink of that voluptuous abyss (a nicety of physiological equipoise comparable to certain techniques in the arts)" (p. 57).

It is significant that Humbert can be near Lolita only by agreeing to a conventional marriage with the mother, just as earlier he married Valeria (whom he calls a "stock character") so as to overcome his abnormal yearning for nymphets. The disgust Humbert feels for these stylized, "normal big" women is the sexual counterpart of his scorn for banal sentiments and hackneyed use of language. His unquenchable desire for Lolita is identified with his search for a mode of expression which is mysterious, tender, alluring, at the same time that it is growing up into the conventional commonplace, for the use of pseudo-artists like Quilty. On one level, then, *Lolita* is a sustained attack on traditional literary banalities; interwoven with this parody of clichés, however, is the search for ecstasy which culminates in the achievement of sincerity and tenderness in human expression. Nabokov presents this search as inseparable from artistic sincerity and tenderness, and therefore his parody of genres is also a mocking exposition of shallow emotionality.

The Foreword to *Lolita* is an obvious parody of the instructive appreciations that commonly preface works on controversial subjects. Thus "John Ray"[9] gravely as-

[9] Diana Butler helpfully identifies the seventeenth-century namesake of John Ray: cf. "Lolita Lepidoptera," p. 63.

sures us that this is a "tragic tale tending unswervingly to nothing less than moral apotheosis." Much of the mock-preface is clearly ridiculous: not only the above invocation of "tragic" respectability, but also the condescending tolerance for Humbert Humbert, even though he is "abnormal" and "not a gentleman," and the insistence on the "general lesson" beneath the morbid details. Finally, "John Ray" patronizingly suggests that "this poignant personal study" should alert us to see beyond the twisted passion of Humbert Humbert to contemporary evils (p. 7).

This Foreword is an example of the versatility of Nabokov's humor. On the surface it is a parody of conventional prefaces, with their slick, serious, "open-minded" evaluations. But Nabokov does not simply endorse the obverse of John Ray's opinions. The preface asserts the moralistic critical cliché that *Lolita* deals with the horrifying misery and consequences of perversion in order to affirm, obliquely, the value of morality, and to show the insidious threat to our ethical beliefs: "In this poignant personal study there lurks a general lesson; the wayward child, the egotistic mother, the panting maniac—these are not only vivid characters in a unique story: they warn us of dangerous trends; they point out potent evils." This is a parody of the insistence of critics that literature is not only a "story" but can be utilized as social commentary and moral guidebook. Yet Nabokov is implying not merely that this novel does nothing of the sort, but that, without knowing it, John Ray is telling the truth: that *Lolita* "warns us of dangerous trends," except that the warning is not moral or social, but rather aesthetic and literary. "The wayward child, the egotistic mother, the panting maniac" are, from an artistic point of view, not social evils, but evils of hackneyed characterization and theme in contemporary novels. Much of

the irony of the preface lies in Ray's obtuseness in failing
to recognize that the same "types" of characters are given
the opposite roles from those which they play in conventional novels.

Nabokov's Afterword to *Lolita*—which has a more
subtle but nevertheless potent element of tongue-in-
cheek discussion ("an impersonation of Vladimir Nabokov talking about his own book")—repudiates John
Ray's declaration that the novel has a "moral" and asserts that the object of the work is to "afford" "aesthetic
bliss." In comparing the modern pornographer with
his eighteenth-century counterpart, Nabokov notes the
"musts" of the twentieth-century work: "Action has to
be limited to the copulation of clichés. Style, structure,
imagery should never distract the reader from his tepid
lust." If these rules are not adhered to, the modern pornographer runs the same risk as a detective story writer:
that "the real murderer may turn out to be, to the fan's
disgust, artistic originality" (p. 284). I contend that the
"real perversion" in *Lolita* is artistic originality, and that
when Nabokov complains of having had to abandon
his "natural idiom," and being forced to do without
"the baffling mirror, the black velvet backdrop, the implied associations and traditions—which the native il-
lusionist, frac-tails flying, can magically use to transcend
the heritage" (p. 289), he is incidentally giving us clues
about his techniques of transcending the "heritage" of
contemporary fiction.

The use of parody as literary criticism is interwoven
with the other themes of *Lolita*; and it is possible, on
one level, to regard the slangy, vulgar, irresistible
nymphet as an embodiment of the possibilities inherent
in the stock "wayward-child" character, or as an example
of how "literary originality" can utilize a moral taboo
for its subject. As I will try to show, moral taboo

merges with literary taboo, and we get the supreme subject of literary originality posing as the main character
of a novel about literary originality.

The parodic style is also an indirect mode of characterizing Humbert. Aside from the frequent statements on
his madness or megalomania by Humbert himself, his
seemingly rational descriptions of his reactions also indicate that he is perennially on the verge of insanity. His
madness is sometimes the comic replica of a literary pose,
as in the scene after he has received Charlotte's love letter:

> After a while I destroyed the letter and went to my room,
> and ruminated, and rumpled my hair, and modeled my purple
> robe, and moaned through clenched teeth and suddenly—
> Suddenly, gentlemen of the jury, I felt a Dostoevskian grin
> dawning (through the very grimace that twisted my lips)
> like a distant and terrible sun. I imagined (under conditions of
> new and perfect visibility) all the casual caresses her mother's
> husband would be able to lavish on his Lolita. . . . "To hold
> thee lightly on a gentle knee and print on thy soft cheek a
> parent's kiss. . . ." Well-read Humbert! (P. 66.)

The techniques of love-making identified with literary
techniques, Humbert's lust described as "the writer's
ancient lust," the scenes of the novel referred to as a
"dream," a "daymare," all point to a level of interpretation on which the action of the novel becomes metaphorical of the act of artistic creation. Indeed, it is possible to
title this level of meaning, as Humbert suggests, "the portrait of the artist as a younger brute" (p. 239). Lolita
herself exists on this plane as an ephemeral, ever-changing
chief character in a projected work by an egomaniacal,
alternately guilt-ridden and triumphant Humbert. Initially she is a potential fictional subject, existing in the
unformed flux of the physical world, whose creation
by Humbert simultaneously involves destruction. The
twelve-year-old Dolores Haze lives in the everyday landscape of suburban America, mediocre and anonymous,

until Humbert, with "a few madhouses behind him" and
his nymphetic obsession before him, decides to invest
her with a fictitious allure and build her into a work of
art. The object of Humbert's search is avowedly illusory,
and he knows that its glow will disappear by the time
he has found and used her. He often compares his wooing
of Lolita to a "game," or a "hunt," and the gradual numb-
ness and unhappiness into which he transfixes Lolita also
suggests the predicament of the artist, trying to capture
his subject in the act of motion but succeeding only in
divesting it of its vitality. Hence the persistent emphasis
on Humbert's guilt, on the fading of Lolita's connection
with everyday life, the growing bitterness and misery
of their cohabitation.

Humbert experiences both pride and agony in seeing
Lolita play tennis. She is used to playing childish games
of volleyball against a neighboring wall, but Humbert
has her take professional lessons in tennis; and watching
her, he has "the teasing delicious feeling of teetering on
the very brink of unearthly order and splendor" (p. 210).
Humbert's obsession for her has forcefully molded the
average Dolly into an "unearthly order" which shuts her
off from the normal life of her contemporaries. Similarly,
a cherished object of emotion may be abstracted and removed from its natural surroundings. Humbert's aesthetic
obsession destroys the object of its attention; he watches
the tennis game "with an almost painful convulsion of
beauty assimilated." But Lolita has become the shell
of her former self: she has a "form" which is "an absolutely perfect imitation of absolutely topnotch tennis,"
without any interest in the actual goal of the game. She
has acquired the flattened, two-dimensional quality of
an abused theme, and Humbert, in retrospect, sees that
"had not something within her been broken by me—not
that I realized it then!—she would have had on the top

of her perfect form the will to win, and would have become a real girl champion" (p. 212). But Humbert has recreated Lolita in his own desire, and this new Lolita is sullenly but irrevocably dependent on him alone: "She had absolutely nowhere else to go."

Yet there remains a tantalizing part of Lolita which is resistant to the process of artistic abstraction, which constantly threatens to grow up and engulf the nymphet part. This stubborn streak is always contemplating escape, and responds shrilly to Humbert's love-making. And it is this streak which Humbert in the end comes to love. It is partly the streak of self-sustaining vitality in fictional characters which transcends and resists even their creator, the author himself.

The struggle between Humbert and Quilty is described as the "silent, soft, formless tussle on the part of the two literati," and the scene has a nightmarish unreality which reflects the state of mind of the dazed Humbert, who is blinded by his artificial world of hallucinatory images. As Lolita is trying to explain her aversion to him, Humbert silently supplies the words for her: "*He* broke my heart. *You* merely broke my life" (p. 254).

The novel abounds in references to literary form and devices, as if the ravages of Humbert's work were strewn all over the creative battlefield. Humbert has "used" the beautiful, trusting, American countryside, and in the process "defiled" it.[10] Charlotte, the faithful "seal," has been eliminated, and Valeria and her husband were made to live as the degraded subjects of a scientific experiment. The bizarre, half-naked character who is found in Hum-

[10] Humbert muses in jail that "our long journey had only defiled with a sinuous trail of slime the lovely, trustful, dreamy, enormous country that by then, in retrospect, was no more to us than a collection of dog-eared maps, ruined tour books, old tires, and her sobs in the night—every night, every night—the moment I feigned sleep" (p. 160).

bert and Rita's bedroom near the end of the book, claims
that Humbert has "purloined" his identity, and he is
renamed at the local asylum as "Humbertson." It is as
if Humbert had toyed with the idea of developing him as
a character, but had finally decided to leave him without
identity. Several other characters are only half-developed:
the neighbor in Ramsdale is simply called Miss Opposite,
and an unnamed celebrity is referred to as Mr. Double-
name (an early hint of Quilty). The main characters are
suggestive of the creative process; their identities and
defining qualities are constantly shifting. Quilty is
amorphously present in Ramsdale, speaks in the dark of
The Enchanted Hunters Inn, and slowly evolves from an
amalgam of Uncle Gustave Trapp to a series of shadowy
figures who trail Humbert in variously colored rented
cars. Even these cars often acquire qualities suggestive of
their driver—as at the Chestnut Crest garage, where "a
red hood protruded in somewhat cod-piece fashion" (p.
196), a reference to Quilty's odious sexuality. Quilty's
artificiality is further emphasized by his nickname,
"Cue." *quelque*

Humbert's theories of sex and of perception reveal a
preoccupation with the intellectual uses of physical phenomena: "It is not the artistic aptitudes that are secondary
sexual characters . . . ; it is the other way around: sex
is but the ancilla of art" (p. 236). His vision is clouded
by the urge to abstract the present and render it timeless: "You know—trying to see things as you will remember having seen them" (p. 81). Thus the flux of
the moment is frozen into its interacting components,
and becomes a disjointed tableau of details. He sees
Charlotte's death in an "actual flash" of "sharp unity,"
but his analytical mind resolves it into a revelation of
"the agent of fate," consisting of "intricacies of the

pattern" (p. 96) which made up the physical event. Humbert's article on the mind proposes "a theory of perceptual time based on the circulation of the blood and conceptually depending . . . on the mind's being conscious not only of matter but also of its own self, thus creating a continuous spanning of two points (the storable future and the stored past)" (p. 237).[11]

Humbert's mind gradually de-emphasizes "matter," and concentrates on a consciousness of its own self. Thus the two spanned points which operate between future and past are intertwined and frequently identified. For example, the shock of finding the tennis court empty suggests "Charlotte's face in death," and this past event is merged with two hypothetical present alternatives which appear as solid realities to Humbert: "I . . . noticed Lo in white shorts receding through the speckled shadow of a garden path in the company of a tall man who carried two tennis rackets. I sprang after them, but as I was crashing through the shrubbery, I saw, in an alternate vision, as if life's course constantly branched, Lo, in slacks, and her companion, in shorts" (p. 149). The alternate vision is not life's course, but rather the alternative suggested by the imagination, or by the process of artistic creation which deliberates between two possible representations of a particular scene. We are frequently given numerous possibilities or versions of a scene, just as we see shifting characteristics of Quilty, Humbert, and Lolita. The total impression is of a story which is in

[11] In the Appel interview, Nabokov remarks that "Imagination is a form of memory. Down, Plato, down, good dog. An image depends on the power of association, and association is supplied and prompted by memory. . . . [Recollection is] that element which creative imagination may use when combining it with later recollections and inventions. In this sense, both memory and imagination are a negation of time." (*Ibid.*, p. 140.)

the act of being composed.[12] Humbert himself is the most intricately developed character, and he is the mainspring of the action. If his vision is prismatic, so is the vision of the author who manipulates him. Thus we have the illusory representation of action as told by Humbert's journal, and the illusory existence of Humbert himself, as created by Nabokov.

The "intricate pattern" of conventional art is sometimes referred to as McFate, whom Humbert is constantly and unsuccessfully trying to outwit. "Precise fate" (p. 96) arranges Charlotte's death, which is actually a demand of the plot of the story, or a demand of the novel convention, to which the tortured Humbert surrenders his ideal passion. As Humbert comes to the end of his narrative, and looks back from the pregnant, ruined Dolly Schiller to the twelve-year-old misty Lolita, he realizes that the artistic process he glorified in the past, "what I used to pamper among the tangled vines of my heart, *mon grand péché radieux*, had dwindled to its essence: sterile and selfish vice" (p. 253). He had imposed his own obsession on the everyday physical world: "Nothing could make my Lolita forget the foul lust I had inflicted upon her. Unless it can be proven to me . . . that in the infinite run it does not matter a jot that a North American girl-child named Dolores Haze had been deprived of her childhood by a maniac, unless this can be proven (and if it can, then life is a joke), I see nothing for the treatment of my misery but the melancholy and very local palliative of articulate art. To quote an old poet:

[12] *Invitation to a Beheading*, Nabokov's most deliberately "unreal" and "daymarish" work, is full of semi-created characters and dialogues, as in Cincinnatus' conversation with the prison director: "Cincinnatus said: 'Kind. You. Very.' (This still had to be arranged.) 'You are very kind,' said an additional Cincinnatus, having cleared his throat."

The moral sense in mortals is the duty
We have to pay on mortal sense of beauty." (P. 258.)

A "mortal," constricted artistic awareness ("sense of beauty") produces a concern with morality. But the imagination which is not bounded by time or moral taboo has a "sense of beauty" which is independent of "reality" or morality. If the act of transforming and creating a nymphet from an ordinary child is retroactively seen by Humbert as a "sterile and selfish vice," it is the vice of the artist's sinister manipulation. Humbert's "sense of beauty" is heightened and purified after he has completed and "lost" his creation. The seventeen-year-old Lolita is no longer an object of obsessive lust ("all *that* I canceled and cursed"), no longer a resurrection of the ideal of the past (Annabel), but loved for herself, as she is in the present. "I insist the world know how much I loved my Lolita, *this* Lolita, pale and polluted, and big with another's child, but still grey-eyed, still sooty-lashed, still auburn and almond, still Carmencita, still mine" (p. 253).

Quilty (perhaps his name denotes the idea of his being a patchwork of a number of characters), as a rival, is a practitioner of thoroughly conventional art. He is a "public" author; he appears in cigarette ads and teenage magazines, and makes pornographic movies. He also "likes little girls," and the prison *Who's Who* informs Humbert that Quilty's "many plays for children are notable," such as *The Little Nymph* (in which Lolita plays the main character in the Ramsdale production). Quilty makes use of art in a cold, calculating way, he has no creative power (significantly, he confesses to Humbert that he did not enjoy Lolita because he is impotent); he uses Lolita for a brief scene and then discards her.

The amorphous figure of Quilty is a threat to the artistic integrity of Humbert's creation. As Humbert realizes that he is being pursued by Lolita's unknown seducer, he knows that the deadly struggle between his conception of art (as passion, lust, agonizing destruction of creator and object) and Quilty's dashing facility is being decided. The difference between the two men is a quality of seriousness and ecstasy, which Humbert sees dramatized in the chase on the highway "between our humble blue car and [his] imperious red shadow—as if there were some spell cast on that interspace, a zone of evil mirth and magic, a zone whose very precision and stability had a glass-like virtue that was almost artistic" (p. 200). Perhaps this is the zone which Humbert unsuccessfully tries to transcend in his attempt to save his ideal of Lolita from becoming crystallized in a standard artistic mode.

When Humbert hears Dolly Schiller identify Quilty as her abductor, he comments: "I, too, had known it, without knowing it, all along. . . . Quietly the fusion took place, and everything fell into order, into the pattern of branches that I have woven throughout this memoir with the express purpose of having the ripe fruit fall at the right moment; yes, with the express purpose of rendering . . . that golden and monstrous peace through the satisfaction of logical recognition, which my most inimical reader should experience now" (p. 248).

The "fusion" should be taking place in the reader's mind: the character of Quilty should merge into Humbert. Humbert supplies the clues for this fusion by emphasizing his own role as artist: "the pattern of branches that _I_ have woven throughout this memoir" (italics added). The pattern has been anticipated and manipulated by Humbert, the "woven branches" are the action, dialogues, and characters of the novel. The stress on the deliberate artistic patterning ("with the express purpose of rendering") and the parody of conventional fictional expectations ("the satisfaction of logical recognition") serve to remind us in the midst of a "realistic" scene that Humbert is writing and arranging the story we are reading. The paradox of "I, too, had known it, without knowing it" might suggest that H.H., for novelistic purposes, had to *pretend* to his readers that he had not all along known about Quilty, or that H.H. here is hinting at his awareness of the omniscient author behind him, who has plotted the story from the start.

Humbert is master of the characters within the scope of his journal. He manipulates them according to his whim—except for the character of Lolita, who obsesses him. His vision reflects the manifold recesses of literary possibility. He ironically sees himself in the pose of the creative artist: "Humbert the Cubus schemed and dreamed—and the red sun of desire and decision (the two things that create a live world) rose higher and higher, while upon a succession of balconies a succession of libertines, sparkling glass in hand, toasted the bliss of past and future nights" (p. 67). His vision is directed at the image of illusion within illusion, as his constant references to mirrors and lakes suggest. His fantasy spans the past and the future. The potentiality of perfection lures him on in his painful affair with Lolita—but her essence, which is rooted in the present, eludes him.

We cannot ascertain whether Quilty is actually following their car, or whether the "clues" of the hotel registers were really diabolically planted by Quilty. What is important is that Humbert is driven to the edge of madness by the effort to preserve Lolita in his own image, and the guilt and shame of his irreparable tampering with her magic serve to point to his inability to attain the perfect literary "equipoise" between her movement in everyday life and her immobile existence in the realm of art. Humbert is perennially toying with shifting scenes and dia-

logues: the enactment of the final murder scene with
Quilty is the amalgam of numerous versions of murders
culled from Humbert's dreams and hallucinations. This
may account for the nightmarish, unreal quality of the
final scene, as if Humbert had not quite decided how
the scene should take place, and is experimenting with a
dummy Quilty to determine the best posture and the most
suitable number of bullets.

Humbert constantly hears unsaid echoes of conversations, and this gives the impression that the unused lines
which he has decided to eliminate from the final version
are still lingering behind the irrevocably "used" ones.
At The Enchanted Hunters Inn, Humbert has a conversation with a still uncreated Quilty, to whom he has decided to give a voice, but not a name or a face. Even
the act of "creating" Quilty's voice is dramatized: "The
rasp of a screwing off, then a discreet gurgle, then the
final note of a placid screwing on. . . . His voice addressed
me: 'Where the devil did you get her?' 'I beg your par-
don?' 'I said: the weather is getting better' " (p. 117).
Humbert mentally adds "stillborn babies" to a motel's
otherwise innocuous list of things not to be flushed in the
toilet; his description of himself fluctuates between Humbert the Wounded Spider and Humbug the Giant Killer.

He is gradually enveloped by the consequences of his
desecration, at first only as a vague hint, later as a per-
petual shadow. Still at the beginning of their romance,
he retroactively sees himself and Lolita in a symbolic
relationship: "She was sprawling and sobbing, and pinch-
ing my caressing hand, and I was laughing happily, and
the atrocious, unbelievable, unbearable, and, I suspect
eternal horror that I know now, was still but a dot of
blackness in the blue sky of my bliss" (p. 154).

Perhaps Quilty serves partly to dramatize Humbert's
ritualistic killing of pseudo-art, which has defiled his own

passionately loved art object. It is not until Humbert decides to kill Quilty that the playwright actually begins
to "exist." Humbert the artist sees that the plot necessi-
tates Quilty's appearance, and "in the methodical manner
on which I have always prided myself, I had been keeping Clare Quilty's face masked in my dark dungeon,
where he was waiting for me. . . . I have no time right now
to discuss the mnemonics of physiognomization" (pp.
264–265). Apparently Humbert does not leave himself
enough time to do a thorough characterization, because
he describes the about-to-be-eliminated Quilty as "this
semi-animated, subhuman trickster" (p. 269).

In sharp contrast to the half-emerging characters
around her, Lolita is described in minute detail: her
smell, her mannerisms, her thigh and arm measurements
are given with meticulous precision. But only too late
does Humbert realize that he has given her no soul, that
in spite of his painstaking artistry he has failed to ap-
preciate her wonder and mystery, and it shocks him to
the border of unconsciousness to think that "I simply did
not know a thing about my darling's mind, and that quite
possibly, behind the awful juvenile clichés, there was in
her a garden and a twilight, and a palace gate" (p. 259).

Humbert's awareness of the peril of his artistic attempt
makes him a jealous guardian of Lolita, both to protect
himself and to keep her from being soiled by the "dirty
children who were her contemporaries." After she has
left him, Humbert finds that she has broken something
in him: "One essential vision in me had withered: never
did I dwell now on possibilities of bliss with a little
maiden, specific or synthetic . . . ; never did my fancy
sink its fangs into Lolita's sisters, far, far away, in the
coves of evoked islands" (p. 235). He is still dominated
by the compulsion to track down Lolita and Quilty, but
he knows that he can derive no happiness from indulging

in his monomania. He has given up the dream of actualiz-
ing the phantoms of the imagination, phantoms which
were initially "perfect, just because the vision was out of
reach, with no possibility of attainment to spoil it by the
awareness of an appended taboo; indeed it may well be
that the very attraction immaturity has for me lies . . .
in the security of a situation where infinite perfections fill
the gap between the little given and the great promised—
the great rosegray never-to-be-had" (p. 241). This description corresponds to Humbert's "pre-dolorian past,"
when the promise of attaining the ideal was made by
Annabel. "Since I sometimes won the race between my
fancy and nature's reality, the deception was bearable.
Unbearable pain began when chance entered the fray and
deprived me of the smile meant for me. . . . The radiant
foreglimpse, the promise of reality, a promise not only
to be simulated seductively but also to be nobly held—
all this, chance denied me—chance and a change to smaller characters" (p. 241). The terminology of drama and
print ("smaller characters"), along with a hint of the
omniscient author's control ("chance"), is used to express
Humbert's sense of the circumscribed nature of his world
and of his imaginative range.

If Humbert sees a "succession of balconies with a succession of libertines" (the libertines being the multiple
reflections of his lustful self, refracted in the process of
re-creation), so Nabokov sees a succession of Humberts
on shifting fictional levels. Gaston, the lovable, harmless
pervert, and Quilty, the witty, vulgar, commercial
nympholept, dramatize extremes of Humbert's varied personality. The novel builds up and undermines its "realistic" illusion, presenting a succession of characters on a
succession of mimetic levels.[13] While Humbert frequently

[13] The shifting aspect of *Lolita* is discussed by several critics,
most suggestively by Carol T. Williams; "Nabokov's Dialectical

appears to be the sole creator of his narrative, various details, acts of McFate, flutterby inserts, and the shadow extending from the Foreword point to the author who created Humbert. Within the narrative sequence of the theme of creation, Humbert, the passionate but minor author, loses control of his main character and becomes a slave to her in the act of abusing her; his lust gives way to tenderness when he realizes that affection is the mainspring of creation. (This realization, which takes place during Humbert's visit to Dolly Schiller, is foreshadowed by the school play in which Lolita acts, though the play is a parodic distortion of the "outer" novel's action.) Whether or not we are to "believe" Humbert's final conversion and declaration of love does not seem to me to be an issue in the novel. The element of surprise, of the contradiction and inconsistency joyfully embraced and passionately asserted, becomes metaphoric of the artist's relationship to his material. Humbert's unconventional obsession is a necessary aspect of imaginative transformation, and his acceptance of his love for the grown-up Lolita provides for his moral apotheosis into the realm of art.

Humbert to the end remains partly destructive and ludicrous (Nabokov's moral condemnation always hovers around Humbert's rhetoric), but he is allowed the saving recognition that feeling is primary and that grace springs from love lavished on illusory or alien objects. On the level of the art theme, *Lolita* deals with the complexities of a fictional world, with certain artistic problems in the portrayal of imaginative reality, a consideration which is already at least once removed from the philosophical problem of perceiving reality. The questions tackled by

Structure," in the Dembo anthology, pp. 176–182, and in greater detail by Alfred Appel, Jr., in *The Annotated Lolita*, both in the far-ranging Introduction and in the painstakingly assembled Notes.

Lolita are artistic, or aesthetic, and the "moral" dilemma is treated in aesthetic terms. Humbert's "vice" is the inexpert artist's brutal treatment of a tantalizingly undeveloped subject, whose fragile soul Humbert has violated. The grossest violation is Quilty's, the commercial artist's, and his crime is so monstrous that it merits the greatest punishment in a novel about artistic creation: he is left deliberately half-created.

What Nabokov, living in his workshop "among discarded limbs and unfinished torsos" (p. 289), attempts to achieve is an artistic triumph related to the basic problem of fiction. Humbert observes that "we are inclined to endow our friends with the stability of type that literary characters acquire in the reader's mind. . . . Never will Emma rally, revived by the sympathetic salts in Flaubert's father's timely tear. Whatever evolution this or that popular character has gone through between book covers, his fate is fixed in our minds. . . . Any deviation in the fates we have ordained would strike us as not only anomalous but unethical" (p. 242). But Humbert, weaving in and out of madness, treating Lolita with alternate cruelty and ecstasy, has no "stability of type." He has been deliberately created to embody the metaphoric perversion and contradictions inherent in the desire to possess and to create. The journal he writes reflects this instability, and we will never know how much of his life was coincidence, how much of it chance, how much of it the cruel machinations of a rival. Whether he is mad or not, whether he imagined the entire story of his affair with Lolita, is not answered by the book. His complexities are the embodiments of artistic problems and of the creative process. His fantasy-life is indistinguishable from his "real" life. The characters he encounters, the conversations he records, cannot be checked against a yardstick of "what really happened." Nabokov, in creating Humbert, has attempted to write a book in which the characters are infinitely fluid, and the action takes place on a "succession" of fictional planes, so that the characters cannot be finally "stilled" or "fixed" as being particular "types," whose fate is sealed forever within the confines of the covers of the book.

Nabokov lightly foregoes the obligation to give us all the necessary information about the characters or the nature of the action. He has "transcended the heritage" of the author's responsibility for providing final answers, or defining the limits of his work. Humbert's obsession is the pursuit of ecstasy through artistic creation. This quest for a pattern within his obsession is conveyed by various metaphors for the act of writing. These metaphors often assume a "realistic" aura, at least momentarily, but eventually they fuse into the creating mind of Humbert. The despair, shame, agony, and tenderness with which Humbert fashions the figure of Lolita is the subliminal journey in the novel. It is a journey through the mind of a mad yet lucid memoirist whose tale reveals artistic as well as emotional agony. In the act of tracing this perverted quest for ecstasy, the omniscient author creates an allusive web beyond his hero's awareness. Artistry and perversion thus enact a quasi-realistic drama of verbal gaiety and emotional intensity. This heightened drama illuminates the undercurrents, both playful and agonizing, of the literary process.

V

PNIN
*Pattern
Broken by Life*

PNIN is a fictional demonstration that the pattern of
life is open to unpredictable variations even when en-
closed within a narrative structure. The novel consists
of a delicate interplay between Pnin as an identity reflected on a fictional pattern and Pnin as a "realistic"
presence capable of escaping the narrator's insistent attention. The brief, unexplained references to the "several"
Pnins, the mysterious confusion about Pnin's alleged
"double," and certain recurrent details in Pnin's life suggest that his identity may be only a temporary fictional
illusion. Victor's painting of a car is an analogue of
this method of characterization: "One way to do it might
be by making the scenery penetrate the automobile. . . .
Now break the body of the car into separate curves and
panels; then put it together in terms of reflections" (p.
97). Thus the car exists as a real object; but while we
are aware of this solid core, what we actually see in the

painting consists of those things which the "shiny" body of the car mirrors. In the same way, the touching and comic dignity of Pnin is partly seen through the tilted planes of the reflections of his past and present.

But the opening moves about the "several Pnins" and the "double" or "Twynn" of Pnin are left undeveloped and unresolved. The narrator seems to be toying with the idea of multiple reflections and doubles (subjects taken rather seriously in the rest of Nabokov's fiction) without, however, integrating this idea into the essential characterization of the main figure. These conventions are invoked in order to emphasize how inappropriate they are in the case of a character who is an "original." The fictional game is overshadowed by the main character; an object of delight and compassion, Pnin is one of Nabokov's most "alive" and touching creations. His immediate vividness is a brilliant achievement attained in spite of a deliberately external point of view. Pnin's intermost feelings are unknown to us; he is indeed the "solus-rex" awaiting rescue from the shores of his own narrative.

The "separate curves and panels" of Pnin's life are assembled by a narrator who has a small but persistent role. He is "the litterateur" who has an affair with Liza, leading her to attempt suicide and subsequently marry Pnin. Liza gives him Pnin's letter of proposal. He meets Pnin at various emigré celebrations, and finally replaces him in his job at Waindell ("Vandal") College. He is acquainted with Eric Wind, Liza's second husband, and he is the guest of Jack Cockerell, the chairman of the English department, who has made a lifetime hobby of parodying Pnin. These various connections and possible sources of information for the narrator are revealed mostly at the end of the novel. It is also made clear that Pnin knows of the narrator's involvement with Liza, and dislikes him. Pnin in fact refuses his offer of assistance and

leaves Waindell so as not to see his rival. As Andrew
Field suggests, "The narrative movement of *Pnin* is the
flight of a character from his author, and, like Gogol's
Akaky Akakievich, Pnin finally succeeds in escaping,
with the help, of course, of the author" (p. 132).

Another possible way of seeing Pnin's relationship to
the narrator is to distinguish between the narrator (the
man whom Pnin resents and finally escapes) and the author (the manipulator who makes the escape possible,
who contains and transcends the narrator in his capacity
for pity). The narrator collects humorous anecdotes about
"freak" Pnin, the author places these anecdotes in the
context of suffering Pnin. As Arthur Mizener demonstrates, the author also conveys to us the fact—unreal-
ized by Pnin—that the day described in Chapter 3 is
Pnin's birthday.[1]

In Nabokov's other novels, the refracted nature of the
main character is made to emphasize the omniscience of
the author, the shifting nature of reality, or the enduring
qualities of art. In *Pnin*, however, the "penetration of the
scenery" serves to point to the hero's isolation, to the
inescapable presence of alien imprints on his vulnerable
sensibility. Beneath the external "planes and curves,"
Pnin is alone and helpless, an exile from his essential self,
a stranger to his surroundings. He expects touchingly
little of life; the impossible possibility of having Liza
again, and the frustrated desire to own the first house he
has ever lived in "all by himself":

To hold her, to keep her—just as she was—with her cruelty,
with her vulgarity, with her blinding blue eyes, with her mis-
erable poetry, with her fat feet, with her impure, dry, sordid,
infantile soul. (Pp. 57–58.)

[1] "The Seriousness of Vladimir Nabokov," Sewanee Review,
76 (1968), 660.

The sense of living in a discrete building all by himself was to Pnin something singularly delightful and amazingly satisfying to a weary old want of his innermost self, battered and stunned by thirty-five years of homelessness.

. . . With grateful surprise, Pnin thought that had there been no Russian revolution, no exodus, no expatriation in France, no naturalization in America, everything—at the best, at the best, Timofey!—would have been much the same. (P. 144.)

In spite of his loneliness and his exile, Pnin rarely feels persecuted or victimized. He is an innocent who is serenely unaware of his precarious position at Waindell or of the hilarity which his eccentricities produce in his colleagues. Liza leaves him again, and he cannot buy the house he covets, but his soul survives these cruel or impersonal blows of life.

Pnin's capacity to endure is dramatized in the aftermath of his housewarming party, at which he has been told by Hagen that he cannot stay at Waindell. After the guests leave, Pnin prepares a "bubble bath" for the dishes, and lovingly places the aquamarine bowl (a present from Liza's son, Victor) in the water. But as he is wiping a nutcracker, he accidentally drops it into the sink, whereupon "an excruciating crack of broken glass followed" (p. 172). The sense of hopeless waste is nearly unbearable: "He looked very old, with his toothless mouth half open and a film of tears dimming his blank, unblinking eyes. Then with a moan of anguished anticipation, he went back to the sink and, bracing himself, dipped his hand deep into the foam. A jagger of glass stung him. Gently he removed a broken goblet. The beautiful bowl was intact" (pp. 172–173).

Our relief at the durability of the bowl overflows into a renewed faith in Pnin's own endurance. This, and the final exit in the small blue sedan, are the last we see of Pnin at Waindell, and the two incidents are clearly connected. In his childlike delight in things, in his inarticulate sorrow, Pnin's soul—like the beautiful bowl- is inviolable. As Pnin remarks about group psychoanalysis (a possible analogue for the literary "confession" in which the author shares his anguish with his readers, or omniscient narration where a victim's soul is bared in public), "Why not leave their private sorrows to people? Is sorrow not, one asks, the only thing in the world people really possess?" (p. 52).

Victor's favorite art teacher, Lake, asserts that "there is nothing more banal and more bourgeois than paranoia," and that "nothing but individual talent mattered" (p. 96). Pnin's own talent is not artistic, but it is entirely individual. He is allowed to escape the narrator, the two identical great trucks "carrying beer," and the pettiness of Waindell. To the last, Pnin remains simultaneously comic and "intact" in his innocence: "wearing a cap with ear flaps and a storm coat," Pnin swings past the narrator and the obstructing truck, and "free at last spurted up the shining road, which one could make out narrowing to a thread of gold in the soft mist where hill after hill made beauty of distance, and where there was simply no saying what miracle might happen" (p. 191). Compared to the ending of *Lolita*, where Humbert is willingly caught and fixed forever in the reflection of himself on the other (sinister) side of the road, Pnin escapes because the "beauty of distance" in which he exists is not only the "refuge of art," but also the miracle of daily life.

The fact that Pnin's "panels and curves" are not simply part of an artistic design, but also reflect the unfathomable deviations of life, is emphasized throughout the novel. Pnin's several heart attacks are described as sensations which detach him "from reality" (p. 19). The first of these attacks, in a park in a strange town, serves as a retrospective mirror into Pnin's childhood. He relives a minor illness during which he is puzzled by a woodcarv- ing near his bed representing "a bridle path felted with fallen leaves, a lily pond, an old man hunched up on a bench, and a squirrel holding a reddish object in its front paws. Timosha, a methodical child, had often wondered what that object could be (a nut, a pine cone?), and now that he had nothing else to do, he set himself to solve this dreary riddle, but the fever that hummed in his head drowned every effort in pain and panic" (p. 23).

Pnin, recalling this incident on the park bench, is him- self the "old man hunched up on a bench," and thus in the vision of a lifeless carving we see the present reality partly mirroring itself. This mirroring and interweaving, with the squirrel as one of its continuing images, will recur in the narrative. The philosophical problem em- bodied in this interior reflection of a past which incor- porates the details of the present is elucidated in the second part of Pnin's recollection of the equally puzzling wallpaper design:

In the vertical plane a combination made up of three different clusters of purple flowers and seven different oak leaves was repeated a number of times with soothing exactitude; but now he was bothered by the undismissable fact that he could not find what system of inclusion and circumscription governed the horizontal recurrence of the pattern. . . . It stood to reason that if the evil designer—the destroyer of minds, the friend of fever—had concealed the key of the pattern with such mon- strous care, that key must be as precious as life itself. . . . [The quest] was grading into delirium. The foliage . . . lost its papery flatness and dilated in depth. . . . And although the witness and victim of these phantasms was tucked up in bed, he was, in accordance with the twofold nature of his sur- roundings, simultaneously seated on a bench in a green and purple park. During one melting moment, he had the sensa- tion of holding at last the key he had sought; but, coming

from very far, a rustling wind . . . confused whatever pattern
Timofey Pnin's surroundings had once had. He was alive
and that was sufficient. (Pp. 23–24.)

In this crucial passage we see Pnin in all of his characteristic attitudes. Puzzled by undecipherable combinations, anguished by the plan of the "evil designer,"
through which the Nazis murdered his childhood sweetheart, Pnin is simultaneously "witness and victim" of
what is happening to him.

In terms of the artistic method of the novel, Pnin's
dimensions alternate between "papery flatness" and the
three-dimensional depth of reality. (As an example of the
former, the image of two people embracing at the Russian colony in New England is depicted as a "couple
placed with easy art on the last page of Pnin's fading
day" [p. 136]. This description literally occurs on the
"last page" of a chapter dealing with Pnin's day, and reminds us that we are reading a book.) But whatever the
pattern which Pnin is on the verge of finding—or rather,
which the author is on the verge of imposing on Pnin's
life—there is finally no systematic recurrence, because
the most significant thing about the hero is that he is
alive. In psychological terms, Pnin is alive because he has
strong feelings; and in literary terms, he is alive because
he is given an air of reality by the author. In order to
maintain this air of reality he cannot be made part of a
system or pattern; he must be allowed to possess at least
the seeming capacity to act freely and unpredictably. The
artifice of *Pnin* mimics the "realistic" convention.

As an endorsement of the statement that being alive is
sufficient, and as a literary joke within the novel, what
Pnin first sees after awakening from the vision on the
bench seems to be a continuation of his childhood memory: "A grey squirrel sitting on comfortable haunches on
the ground before him was sampling a peach stone. The

wind paused, and presently stirred the foliage again"
(pp. 24–25). Here is the "real-life" solution to what the
reddish object was that the squirrel was holding in its
paws, and the wind stirring the foliage "again" repeats
the event in the childhood delirium. The foliage in the
park is seen through multiple illusory mirrors. Pnin as a
child had imagined that the wallpaper foliage had come
to life; he now recreates that initially imagined scene. The
"actual" foliage in the park reflects the memory of the
imagined foliage, and it has been placed there by the
author as a parallel to the original. A vision which has
occurred on one imaginative plane is repeated on another; the illusory childhood breeze stirring a wallpaper
foliage has become a "real" breeze in a "real" foliage in
Pnin's present life.

A similar instance of Pnin searching for a "key" to a
pattern, thinking he has almost found it, and being interrupted by an event from his empirical existence (a squirrel, of course), occurs after he has seen Liza off:

> All of a sudden he thought: If people are reunited in heaven
> (I don't believe it, but suppose), then how shall I stop it from
> creeping upon me, over me, that shriveled, helpless, lame
> thing, her soul? But this is the earth, and I am, curiously
> enough, alive, and there is something in me and in life——
> He seemed to be quite unexpectedly (for human despair sel-
> dom leads to great truths) on the verge of a simple solution
> of the universe but was interrupted by an urgent request. A
> squirrel under a tree had seen Pnin on the path. (P. 58.)

The "simple solution" which Pnin is on the verge of,
seems to be similar to the conclusion of his first heart
attack, that being alive is "sufficient." Pnin's speculations are curiously like V.'s finding in *Sebastian Knight*,
that "the hereafter may be the full ability of consciously
living in any chosen soul." But just as the "secret truth"
of *Sebastian Knight* is something other than this discov-

ery, and lies in the emotional impact of art, the "solution"
in *Pnin* lies in the uniqueness of the self. Liza's soul "on
earth" cannot creep upon Pnin because there is "something" in him, and "in life," which shields his fragile
consciousness. The search for the "real" Sebastian leads
to a merging of narrator, subject, and author; Pnin's
quest leads to a separation and elucidation of his discrete
identity.

The recollections incurred by Pnin's heart attack tend
to induce a "melting" of his consciousness with other
selves (his childhood self, and the "ghosts" associated
with his childhood). But experience in *Pnin* is insistently
"two-fold": a present reality exists on one side of the
imaginative mirror, and this reality—"something in life"
—recalls him from the obsession of the past. If the retrospective visions involve a kind of "communion" and
"divestment" of individuality, the narrator describes the
opposite experience—that of present reality—as having
"the main characteristics of . . . discreteness. . . . Man
exists only insofar as he is separated from his surroundings" (p. 20). The appearance of the squirrel which punc-
tuates Pnin's musings about being "alive" reminds the
hero of his "discreteness" from his surroundings, of his
role as not only "victim" of his fantasies but also "witness" to a live world. But present reality can be almost as
much a source of sorrow as past losses; Liza's joyfully
anticipated visit turns out to be a cunning scheme. In the
subsequent squirrel episode, the rodent's behavior seems
to mirror Liza's opportunism:

The intelligent animal climbed up to the brim of a drinking
fountain and, as Pnin approached, thrust its oval face towards
him with a rather coarse spluttering sound, its cheeks puffed
out. Pnin understood and after some fumbling he found what
had to be pressed for the necessary results. Eying him with

contempt, the thirsty rodent forthwith began to sample the
stocky sparkling pillar of water, and went on drinking for a
considerable time. "She has fever, perhaps," thought Pnin,
weeping quietly and freely, and all the time politely pressing
the contraption while trying not to meet the unpleasant eye
fixed upon him. Its thirst quenched, the squirrel departed
without the least sign of gratitude. (P. 58.)

The childhood combination on the lifeless woodcarving
has become an animated scene in the present. The details
and the action are slightly distorted—as if blurred by the
new perspective—the lily pond is now a fountain, the
riddle of the "reddish object" has been solved, and Pnin
is not "hunched up on a bench" but hunched up and
crying near the fountain. Thus the "discreteness" of
"life" from inanimate surroundings is asserted, at the
same time that the continuity between life and the imagination is suggested by the repetition of certain details.

The image of the squirrel reappears twice more in the
narrative. While walking to the library, Pnin notices that:

An elliptic flock of pigeons, in circular volitation, soaring
gray, flapping white, and then gray again, wheeled across
the limpid, pale sky, above the College library. A train whistled
afar as mournfully as in the steppes. A skimpy squirrel dashed
over a patch of sunlit snow, where a tree trunk's shadow, olive-
green on the turf, became grayish-blue for a stretch, while
the tree itself, with a brisk, scrabbly sound, ascended, naked,
into the sky, where the pigeons swept by for a third and last
time. The squirrel, invisible now in a crotch, chattered, scold-
ing the delinquents who would pot him out of his tree. (P. 73.)

The balance of this passage is so delicate that we do not
know whether Pnin actually sees a squirrel, or whether
the image is evoked by the memory of the "steppes," and
the lovely play of shadows and colors. The Pninization
of the rodent in the last sentence personalizes the image
by humanizing the motivation for the chattering sound

(like the statement "Perhaps she has fever" in the previous squirrel scene). The squirrel remains "invisible" for the rest of the novel, except for a postcard which Pnin sends to Victor, which pictures the "Gray Squirrel" and informs us that the derivation of "squirrel" is the Greek word for "shadow-tail" (p. 88). Since the appearance of the squirrel has been surrounded by shadows, delicate grays, and Pnin's heart attack (which he describes as "a shadow behind the heart"), the derivation explains the pattern of the squirrel image. The squirrel is, literally, one of the *shadows* which *tails* Pnin from his childhood. The derivation charmingly fits into the symbolic and narrative use to which this simultaneously imagined and real object has been put.

The slight and deliberate distortion of detail, which I have noted in connection with the previous squirrel scene, is especially striking in the treatment of the incident which appears at the beginning and the end of the novel. The first chapter starts with Pnin bound for Cremona, discovering that he is on a wrong train, but finally assembling his luggage and notes and giving his lecture without any slips. The last paragraph of the novel presents the narrator with Cockerell (Pnin's devoted mimic), who is preparing to tell "the story of Pnin rising to address the Cremona Women's Club and discovering that he had brought the wrong lecture" (p. 191). Field, the only critic to notice the discrepancy between the story we read in the beginning and the one Cockerell is about to relate, offers the following possible explanations: "Has the narrator reordered Cockerell's story . . . so that the humorous incident would be less banal, or is Cockerell merely repeating a second-hand, garbled account (wrong lecture instead of wrong train)? . . . Both versions, at any rate, are set down by the narrator who can be trusted when, as in this instance, he indicates that he is not to be trusted."[2]

I think that a more plausible explanation of the discrepancy (on the basis of the technique observable in the squirrel episodes) lies in the theory of "pattern broken by life." The author has implied that Pnin's experiences could be systematically plotted, but that any such attempt is bound to break down in the case of a character who is so overpoweringly "alive." In the first chapter the narrator tells us of his predilection for certain conventions: "Had I been reading about this mild old man, instead of writing about him, I would have preferred him to discover, upon his arrival to Cremona, that his lecture was not this Friday but the next. Actually, however, he not only arrived safely but was in time for dinner, . . . , juggling three papers, all of which he had stuffed into his coat" (p. 26). The narator's protestations of veracity are of course part of a fictional convention, but in the case of *Pnin* these protestations simply reinforce the dramatically felt "lifelikeness" of the main character. Theoretically, two alternate possibilities exist (one proposed by the narrator: wrong day; and another by Cockerell: wrong lecture), but the "real" incident on the wrong train overrules both of its shadows by the sheer fact of its having already happened in the first scene of the

[2] Field, *Nabokov*, p. 135. Stegner is unaware of all factual discrepancies both here and in other episodes, and asserts that "[the narrator] does not appear to be a distorting refractor of the events he relates" (p. 97). Ambrose Gordon, whose thesis about the novel is that "Nabokov's success lies in his decomposition of the figure of the Banished Man into its dual components of the Exile and the Alien" ("The Double Pnin," in *Nabokov*, ed. L. S. Dembo, p. 148), notices the questionable use of the myth of Odysseus, but not the details of the ending. Gordon's remark on Cockerell's story is that we are given a "parody Pnin continuing his ghostly life" (p. 156).

novel. As Pnin might say, there is something "in life" which admits only a single set of factual details.

Although there might be a merging or a bifurcation of details in a novel about artistic technique (which means most of Nabokov's other novels), *Pnin* is concerned with showing a deviation from fictional patterns into lifelike patterns, and therefore records the quest for the "true" details which constitute an "actual" life. After Pnin— who is literally the "life" of the novel—has departed, Cockerell, who resembles and impersonates Pnin, repeats the empty gestures of Pninisms. Here we perceive rigidly systematic mimicry which lacks the individual artistry capable of delightful surprises. In *Pnin*, being alive is "sufficient," but being an imitation is not. The hero of the novel escapes into the "soft mist," while Cockerell is described as having substituted himself as "his own victim for that of the initial ridicule." Cockerell and Pnin thus metaphorically change places; the former remains at Waindell, trapped in the Pnin-mold he himself has created, while the latter, with unpredictable penchant for individuality, drives off on the "shining road" of his intact identity. Perhaps discrete identity in a Nabokov novel can only be achieved by escape from the double. Nabokov's other characters are in constant search of their double, as a way of capturing or destroying something sinister. But Pnin simply throws the burden of banal mimicry on Cockerell. A pattern of parodic doubling is replayed in the end with a liberated Pnin riding toward ordinary life and his compulsive double imprisoned in a literal fictional lie.

VI

BEND SINISTER
The
Pattern of Concentric Circles

BEND SINISTER is ostensibly a "political" novel about the encroachments of a police state on the life of a philosophy professor, Adam Krug. Krug's former schoolmate, The Toad, has recently come into power as the head of the quasi-Nazi/Communist Ekwilist party. A well-known thinker whose wife has just died as the novel begins, and whose son is later brutally murdered at a state asylum, Krug is courted, cajoled, and threatened by the state which is anxious to secure his support. On the political level the story depicts the integrity of a humane man confronted with mindless tyranny. But interwoven with the political plot, *Bend Sinister* presents the image of the author manipulating a dreamer in the midst of a nightmare. A recurrent suggestion is that the fictional surface reflects widening circles (as Nabokov's introduction informs us, "Krug" means "circle" in Russian). Within these circles, different levels or boundaries of reality are circumscribed. The plot moves from omniscient author and dream-producer to philosopher diarist and dreamer, to political tyrant and cartoon character, in receding ripples of vividness.

The world of the novel is simultaneously inhabited by traditionally realistic objects and descriptions, by the comments and mental processes of Krug and his creator, and by the literary allusions which permeate the whole. The main subject and the inner focus (or Phokus) of the plot is the artistic imagination combining and recombining its themes. The involutions of the action constantly direct us toward the dual process of Krug creating his world, encircled by the author creating Krug and his world. Through this dual process space and time, affection and intellect, are collapsed into each other as aspects of literary technique, and death is disinfected of its horror by being rendered as a problem of fictional representation.

The structure of *Bend Sinister* radiates outward from a central consciousness to interlocking patterns. The solace of pattern perceived by Krug is a pattern strategically placed by the author. Krug, in his turn, perceives, and thereby creates, analogous patterns. The concentric and frequently merging circles are waves of imaginative fancy, whose "reality" is the feel of the sensuous artistic texture we are following. This texture is allusive both in respect to external literary references and in respect to the continuous, self-referential web of the unfolding tale. The political theme is one of the outer thematic circles which is incorporated into the main theme of the movement. Politics is shown in perspective as intermittent and minor material for the workings of the artist's imagination. The play elements of *Bend Sinister* suggest that the novel is a stage setting for a theatre of the mind, where an action combining abstract ideas, dramatic characters, stage directions, and a mental landscape (Omigod Lane, Lake Malheur) is being produced by the author.

As part of the cast, yet duplicating the creative process of the author, Krug shapes the ideas and characters within his range. Krug's glimpse of a couple at his doorstep illuminates his faculty of forming characters, connecting them to literary echoes and then joining his author in a leap into fantasy: "Close up, close up! In the farewell shadows . . . an American football player, stood . . . with a sketchy little Carmen— . . . she slipped under his door-holding arm and after one backward glance from the first landing ran upstairs trailing her wrap with all its constellation—Cepheus and Cassiopeia, and Polaris the snowflake on the grizzly fur of the Cub, and the swooning galaxies—those mirrors of infinite space *qui m'effrayent*, Blaise, as they did you" (pp. 58–59). The embracing couple are the unformed shadows of the cast of the novel: Krug later imagines his son as a football player (p. 173), and the maid Mariette develops from the Carmen figure. "Blaise" is Blaise Pascal (from whose *Pensées* the refracted line originates: "Le silence éternel de ces espaces infinis m'effraie"). The creation of an imaginary couple and the description of the girl's wrap widen into a verbal approximation of infinite space, demonstrating the rules of the Nabokovian fictional realm where anything which can be imagined is real— be it character, object, or idea.

The circularity of patterning within the novel is observed partly by the reader and partly by his fictional stand-in, Krug. In the course of the first bridge scene, Krug notices that the philistine grocer starts "running in circles around Krug, he ran in widening circles and imitated a railway engine: . . . Parody of a child—my child" (p. 21). The entire scene is probably Krug's nightmare, and therefore the grocer is a figment of his imagination. This relationship is literalized by the fictional character circling around his creator, who recognizes that the figure is a comic, mental distortion of his son David (who later imitates a railway engine for Krug). The dream state, an analogue to the creative realm, sometimes uses the materials of our awake consciousness to shape the figures of the imagination. In the same scene, Krug walks back and forth on the bridge, reflecting that it is "not a bridge but an hourglass which somebody keeps reversing, with me, the fluent fine sand, inside" (p. 19). This image is a dazzling compression of fictional space and fictional time into a single medium, the medium of artistic technique which "somebody" (the omniscient author) manipulates to give the illusion of space and time. Just as the grocer circles around Krug in order to lend reality to Krug's bridge-dream, so Krug circles around the author to provide a physical and chronological depth to the action. The other characters are ranged concentrically around Krug's creating mind, and the plot also moves around repeated images, stage settings, and frames which surround Krug himself.

The novel often gives us a series of speculations, disjointed notes, or a look at possible themes, as if the work were in the process of being written. In the description of Krug's "odds and ends for an essay" (pp. 143–146), we are shown a cinematic flash of an author amidst his scattered tools and undigested ideas. In the scene of Krug receiving the messenger who brings "a meat pie, a rice pudding, and [Mariette's] adolescent buttocks" (p. 151), we get a list of novelistic props whose comic effect springs from the reminder that a dinner or a part of a human anatomy are equally impersonal components in a fictional landscape. Sometimes the author pretends that he is translating the novel from a proto-Russian original, and that he is having difficulty deciphering the meaning of the text: "[Here the long hand of life becomes extremely illegible.] . . . [witnesses among whom was his own something or other ('inner spy'? 'private detective'? The sense is not at all clear)]" (p. 207, punctuation in the original). There are several literary references here: the idea of translating from an original may be an echo of *Don Quixote*'s Moorish manuscript (where Cervantes too was parodying a convention), and the "inner spy" or "private detective" is a translation of "sogliadatai," the title of a novella Nabokov wrote in 1930 (later translated into English under the title *The Eye*).

The suggestion of a work in progress or a journal is reinforced by the sudden shifts from nightmare to "reality," from first to third-person narration, from play-effects to philosophical speculation to epistolary description. Alternate versions of the same scene (as in Krug's interview with Paduk), stage directions ("describe bedroom," a direction which in this instance is comically disregarded because a character begins to speak before the author has gotten around to the description), and recurring scenery (such as the tunnel and the courtyard, which appear in the school scenes, the nursery, and the Quist interview), serve to remind us that the work is a deliberate artifice. There is constant movement in and out of the minds of Krug and the author, with frequent mergings of the two. The occasional stylistic comments ("old-fashioned simile," p. 82) not only contribute to the breaking up of the illusion of reality, but also suggest the pleasures of verbal and aesthetic awareness.

Krug's ideas, especially on time, seem deliberately fused with the author's comments on the relation of his themes to the overall structure of the novel. Krug writes about "infinite consciousness" and of the strange fact that our nonexistence before birth does not terrify us, whereas the possibility of nonexistence after death is agonizing: "What we are now trying (unsuccessfully) to do is to fill the abyss we have safely crossed with terrors borrowed from the abyss in front, which abyss is borrowed from the infinite past. Thus we live in a stocking which is in the process of being turned inside out, without our ever knowing for sure to what phase of the process our moment of consciousness corresponds" (pp. 176–177). The "process" refers to time, to a life lived and experienced as a series of events leading to death, or perhaps leading back (being "turned inside out") to the same state as the prenatal one. While our "consciousness" imagines that we are progressing toward a hitherto unknown nothingness, this impression may be illusory, and we may be returning on an arc which we have earlier traversed without being aware of it.

Thus time may be other than a dimension to which we attribute the same linear, ever-changing quality which our lives have. Time may be an envelope surrounding our experience, and experience itself a circle which returns us to its starting point. *Bend Sinister* is itself in a way like a stocking being turned inside out; the chronological act of reading does not necessarily correspond to a development in the character or consciousness of its hero, or to the logical progression of its plot. The story and the consciousness of Krug is being revealed in the act of being turned inside out. This structural principle is not a systematic reversal or regression of events, but a process which, through its whimsicality and its unexpected turns, reinforces the impression of uncertainty, and reminds us that we cannot predict what aspect of the story we will read next. Krug—or the author—sometimes re-experiences scenes which took place before the action of the plot. Olga's car accident with the doe, one of the many frames in the novel, is told by both Ember (p. 33) and Krug (pp. 207–208). These frames (which include not only the puddles but also the two bridge scenes) underline the suggestion that the beginning and end of time may coincide, with only slight distortions.

If fictional illusion is a reflection of a general pattern of events, then the forward movement is no more than a deception due to a leap of consciousness. The novel reminds us of this possibility partly through deliberate patterns of recurrence, partly through events being imagined by Krug when he has no proof that they ever occurred (as in his description of Olga taking a moth in and out of a house). Krug's "scenes" often jumble and combine events as fate or the artistic process might—such as the "theme" of his school days, with Olga's death superimposed and mixed with the political doctrines and history of Ekwilism. The author tirelessly reminds us that the fictional development is illusory. The events we have experienced are summarized, the present scene is projected into the future: Krug "imagines himself at some point recalling this particular moment. He, Krug, was sitting beside Ember's bed, . . . Krug had recently lost his wife" (p. 113). Toward the end of the novel the action is recapitulated and the hero reintroduced: "He was a big heavy man. . . . He had lost his wife in November. He had taught philosophy. He was exceedingly virile. His name was Adam Krug" (p. 179).

Thus there is a repeated, teasing suggestion that Krug is not only the main character of the novel but also its author. (For similar elements in the Nabokov canon we can turn to Sebastian Knight, John Shade, and the undisguised example of Humbert Humbert.) In his study, the frustrated Krug, surrounded by his notes, is attempting to write a book which is still "unknown" to him, "except for a vague, shoe-shaped outline" (p. 146). In a special edition of *Bend Sinister*, Nabokov helpfully lists the occurrences of the "puddle" in the novel.[1] The image seen in the beginning is "an oblong puddle set in the coarse asphalt; like a fancy footprint filled to the brim with quicksilver; like a spatulate hole through which you can see the nether sky" (p. 7). The final puddle sums up the pattern within the novel of a basic shape filled anew with each rain, yet retaining its essential outline: "An oblong puddle invariably acquiring the same form after every shower because of the constant spatulate shape of a depression in the ground. Possibly, something of the kind may be said to occur in regard to the imprint we leave in the intimate texture of space" (p. 222).

The oblong, spatulate, kidney-shaped, shoe-shaped depression is the projected structure which faces Krug when he is trying to write his book. Thus, halfway through the novel, in a deliberately jumbled chronological sequence, Krug is shown in his study as he is just beginning to compose the book we are reading. (In a similar structural design, we are shown John Shade finishing his poem and returning his volume of Shade's *Poems* to its shelf, and Sebastian Knight, sprawled out in his room, halfway through the novel, and telling someone that he is not dead, but has just finished writing his book, probably the book we are in the process of reading.) The "depression in the ground" may be each author's unique "imprint," the individual imaginative slant, which fills up with particular fictional raindrops and reflects the passing images of the author's fancy. Krug about to write a work with a shoe-shaped outline, and the novel full of shoe-shaped outlines filled in with faces and scenes, suggests a receding fictional reality, where Krug may be the author of the entire novel, or an

[1] Time Reading Program Special Edition (New York, 1964), p. xiv. To Nabokov's list I would add Lake Malheur, an enlarged form of the same imprint.

author created and manipulated by a more powerful arm
behind him.

There are further hints that the entire novel is a work
that Krug is writing, "combining dim dreams with the
scholarly precision of memory" (p. 61). The beginning
of Chapter 5 ambiguously describes an imagined plot
in literary, psychological, and play-like terms: "It bris-
tled with farcical anachronism; it was suffused with a
sense of gross maturity (as in *Hamlet* the churchyard
scene); its somewhat meagre setting was patched up
with odds and ends from other (later) plays; . . . Nat-
urally, the script of daytime memory is far more subtle
in regard to factual details, since a good deal of cutting
and trimming and conventional recombination has to be
done by the dream producers" (p. 60). Scene and critical commentary are chronologically reversed here. The
subject of the description, "it," refers to the remembrance of childhood which follows, a remembrance into
which details of Krug's later life and an account of the
history and ideas of Ekwilism are incorporated. The
"script of daytime memory" may be synonymous with
the more realistic details of the novel, and the nighttime
memory may be the more grotesque political nightmare.

Another hint that Krug is reliving and recombining
the characters of his plot, even in the seemingly "realistic" hospital corridor and academic meeting, is given
while Krug is observing the head nurse: "With her faded
blue eyes and long wrinkled upper lip she resembled
someone he had known for years but could not recall—
funny. . . . The person (male?) whom she resembled
peered out of the mist and was gone before he could
identify her—or him" (p. 10). At the faculty conference
later, "old President Azareus came at a quick pace, his
arms open, his faded blue eyes beaming in advance, his
long upper lip quivering—— 'Yes, of course—how stupid

of me,' thought Krug, the circle in Krug, one Krug in another one" (p. 40). Thus the same character is cast in both female and male roles on the level of artistic composition; or, in terms of the dream-play, the dreamer recognizes that one or both of these characters is created from a "real-life" acquaintance slightly distorted. (This process resembles in miniature Shade's creation of Charles Kinbote who imagines himself to be King Charles Xavier, from the model of the probably "real" Russian scholar Botkin.)

We do not know whether either or both of these scenes are dreamed by Krug (as he might be dreaming the farcical signing of the pass on the bridge—and we are told is dreaming the second bridge scene). But, in either case, the character amalgamation serves to remind us that both scenes are woven of the same imaginative fabric, rather than being "realistic" descriptions of autonomous characters. The phrase "the circle in Krug" is identical with "one Krug in another one" (since "Krug" means circle in Russian), but its repetition and emphasis at this moment of recognition of a character pattern points to Krug as artist, an independent, self-enclosed identity of a fictional Krug within the writer of the entire novel.

The technique of reminding the reader of the self-referential, illusory quality of the action is repeated at the bridge. The "fat soldier" guarding the bridge, *"who seemed to be the leader of the group,"* is named Gurk (Krug in reverse) and when the grocer asks what name to sign on his pass, the soldiers suggest "Gurk." The novel ranges through Krug's entire life, from boyhood to maturity, and some characters may be dramatizations of the younger Krug as he appears to the imagination of the older, artist Krug. For instance, at the house of President Azareus, Krug suddenly sees that "unchallenged and unsought, a plump pale pimply adolescent entered a dim classroom and looked at Adam who looked away" (p. 47). This disjointed appearance places the mentally visualized younger self on the same fictional plane as the ostensibly "realistic" faculty meeting.

Krug, or "the circle in Krug" (the authorial self) frequently writes or thinks as if his work were in the process of being written—as in the bridge scene: "He had thick (let me see) clumsy (there) fingers" (p. 11). The professor of French speaks English "like a Frenchman in an English book," except "when the author gets bored by the process—or forgets," and then he speaks standard English until "the author remembers again" (p. 39). During Krug's interview with Paduk there are many farcical and deliberately unrealistic details: the messages (one delivered by a parrot) from Paduk's advisers on etiquette, the initial dialogue revoked ("No, it did not go on quite like that"), the re-doing of Paduk's physiognomy by a mortician ("He was a little too repulsive to be credible"), and the stage directions by the author ("It is not a difficult part, but still the actor must be careful . . ."). In one of these stage directions, the author surfaces in order to summarize the action, to reassure the reader of his reliability, and momentarily to contemplate an alternative action: "Thus? Or perhaps in some other way? Did Krug really glance at the prepared speech? And if he did, was it really as silly as all that? He did; it was" (p. 141).

The theatrical and fictional elements of the scene are further emphasized when Paduk intermittently assumes Renaissance rhetoric ("Nay, do not speak. . . . Prithee, go."), Krug is called "my favorite character," and the stage directions state the manner in which the speech should be returned to Paduk. Then in a sudden shift the author suggests that the scene and the men are "real,"

not staged: "But [Krug and Paduk] were clumsy and
cross men, and [Paduk's military and medical experts],
. . . too, were not acting" (p. 141). The scene is
thus given an intermittent effect of "reality" by the
playwright-manager, with occasional intrusions and playful details which bare the skeleton of the artifact.

The basic proposition and structure of the novel shows
the "imprint" of one of Krug's philosophical outlines:

We shall imagine then a prism or prison where rainbows are
but octaves of ethereal vibrations and where cosmogonists
with transparent heads keep walking into each other and
passing through each other's vibrating voids while, all around,
various frames of reference pulsate with Fitz-Gerald con-
tractions. Then give a good shake to the telescopoid kaleidoscope (for what is your cosmos but an instrument containing
small bits of coloured glass which, by an arrangement of
mirrors, appear in a variety of symmetrical forms when rotated—mark: when rotated) and throw the damned thing
away. (P. 158.)

This is an image of the fictional world as a prism of
various gradations and colors of illusory arcs, or as a
"prison" where the writer's imagination tries to order,
restrain, and rehabilitate (literally endow with clothes)
the naked themes. Earlier, Krug had repeatedly called
David, the son whom he adores, "my rainbow" (p. 149),
and perhaps the "octaves of ethereal vibrations" are the
strong emotional attachments which are dramatized in
the novel as Krug's love for his son. The fictional world
is then examined from various points of view, from
various emotional and temporal perspectives (fear,
agony, love, courage, as well as shifts between childhood
games and political pressure), and details are made to
mirror and slightly distort other details. The "bits of
coloured glass" (the vividly realized characters and
scenes) alternate with abstract themes, there is a "rotation" of speakers, of emotional distance, and of artistic

technique. The "good shake" destroys the imaginary character of Krug and his world. In the end of the novel, the parable or extended metaphor is crumpled up, the author wipes away the painted surface, and appears, writing the novel we are reading.

When Krug is in jail toward the end of the novel, the fictional world is steadily thinning, and when he listens to the noises of the jail he hears "the cautious crackling of a page which had been viciously crumpled and thrown in the wastebasket and was making a pitiful effort to uncrumple itself and live just a little longer" (p. 215). The crumpled paper foreshadows the ending where the author is shown "among the chaos of written and re-written pages" (p. 221). The discarded page also resembles the soon-to-be-discarded character Krug, who "lives" only as a pattern or image on paper. Another pattern projected by the author-within-Krug through his philosophical musings contains the thematic outline of the entire novel: "The 'common-sense' affair had turned out to be the gradual digging of a pit to accommodate pure smiling madness" (p. 159).

The semi-realistic details, and the illusion of solid, rational character presented by Krug of himself, in the end suddenly culminate in his benign, liberating madness. This quotation may be another hint of Krug's authorship, since it suggests that he has deliberately designed his madness as part of the fabric of his work (as Shade deliberately plans his death), and that here we see him looking back at the finished structure as we have already seen him (p. 146) at the opposite extreme, with the still "unknown" work which has as yet only a "shoe-shaped outline."

But outlines and structures are philosophical abstractions until they are filled in with specific images and patterns. These specifics are in turn related to Krug's "problems" concerning time and death. During an early scene, returning from the hospital, he muses about Olga's death. On the parapet of the bridge his hand palpates "a certain pattern of roughness," a furrow, a knob, and a hole. The sudden perception of the pattern is then related to his life with Olga:

On this particular night, just after they had tried to turn over to me her purse, her comb, her cigarette holder. I found and touched this—a selected combination, details of the bas-relief. I had never touched this particular knob before and shall never find it again. This moment of conscious contact holds a drop of solace. The emergency brake of time. Whatever the present moment is, I have stopped it. Too late. In the course of our, let me see, twelve, twelve and three months, years of life together, I ought to have immobilized by this simple method millions of moments. . . . What happened to her would perhaps not have happened, had I been in the habit of stopping this or that bit of our common life, prophylactically, prophetically, letting this or that moment rest and breathe in peace. Taming time. Giving her pulse respite. Pampering life, life—our patient. (Pp. 16–17.)

This passage brings together the main philosophic themes of the novel: time, death, and the solace of conscious contact with a fleeting pattern. The present can be stopped by an awareness of some configuration in daily life, here a touch of palpable shapes. Neither the past nor the future can duplicate this awareness, because the pattern is unique and its effect unpredictable. When Krug is saying goodnight to his son later, he observes "a combination of three tiny brown spots, birthmarks, on the faintly flushed cheek near the nose [which] recalled some combination he had seen, touched, taken in recently—what was it? The parapet" (p. 29). The recollection is arbitrary, personal, and triggered by an emotional association. Aside from the tri-vial pattern of the combinations, the parapet's furrow, knob, and hole resemble David's birthmarks only in giving solace, providing pleasure, in circling back to the individual perceiver. Observed or felt details assert the presence of a throbbing sensibility, a live consciousness which is in itself an "emergency brake" on both time and death. A sinister shadow of this pattern recurs in the spy-seductress Mariette's birthmark and love-bites (p. 181).

The stopping of time may be temporary, but nevertheless the imaginative selection refutes the indifferent onrush of experience and renders "common life" in a heartbreakingly vivid combination. The mind, perceiving and transforming details, in a sense creates life through its perceptions and its language. Thus Krug speculates that his wife Olga might have remained alive if he had "stopped" the events of their life through a union of memory and imagination. Krug seems to suggest that her death might have been prevented ("prophylatically") by storing up fixed moments of their past for the future ("prophetically")—thereby providing a new timeless medium where ever-present moments combine to form a continuity outside the conventional notions of time and death. If life is "our patient," "she" dies when its component vivid "bits" are forgotten, blurred, or unnoticed. *Bend Sinister* is an "indictment of totalitarianism" in illustrating that the perceptive, conscious sensibility is a unique, self-sufficient "circle" isolated from the "mud" of enforced sameness and banality. Krug's concern with those whom he loves, with philosophy and its problems of time and death, with finding patterns of solace in fleeting moments, are all acts of implicit "insubordination" which cannot be moulded or repressed by any political system.

If time can be stopped by a sudden awareness of a pattern, perhaps the conventional sequence of past, present, and future is also illusory and can be rejuggled.

During the faculty meeting in Chapter 4, the professor of modern history discusses events of history in terms of time: "As with so many phenomena of time, recurrent combinations are perceptible as such only when they cannot affect us any more—when they are imprisoned so to speak in the past, which *is* the past just because it is disinfected. To try to map our tomorrows with the help of data supplied by our yesterdays means ignoring the basic element of the future which is its complete non-existence" (p. 44). The perspective which allows the perception of a combination to resemble another combination places the first occurrence in the past, and the recurrent combination in the present. The recognition of the similarity is thus necessarily temporal, since recurrence suggests a process in a sequence of time. But, conversely, if "recurrent combinations" continue to "affect" us both as events and emotions in themselves, and as part of an imaginative continuity, then the combinations are not "disinfected" of feeling, and therefore they remain part of our "present" consciousness. This manner of confronting history is similar to Krug's way of "stopping time" on the bridge, just as his final madness is a liberation from time, and a partial return to childhood.

Krug's speculations about death are rooted in considerations of time and consciousness. But all such speculations are muddled by mystery and uncertainty:

What is more important to solve: the 'outer' problem (space, time, matter, the unknown without) or the 'inner' one (life, thought, love, the unknown within) or again their point of contact (death)? For we agree, do we not, that problems *as* problems do exist even if the world be something made of nothing within nothing made of something? Or is 'outer' and 'inner' an illusion too, so that a great mountain may be said to stand a thousand dreams high and hope and terror can be as easily charted as the capes and bays they helped to name? (P. 160.)

Since the definition of the "problem" is blurred by the possibility that all objects may exist in purely emotional terms, the solution may lie in the merging of all points of contact into the "dreams," "hope," and "terror" of the philosopher.

But even if our emotions contain all objects, we cannot speak of abstract problems or feelings without the texture of a visualized scene. Krug admits to being "a slave of images" (p. 161), and his writings about death illustrate the process of theoretical illusion widening out into a concrete image: "To seek perfect knowledge is the attempt of a point in space and time to identify itself with every other point; death is either the instantaneous gaining of perfect knowledge (similar say to the instantaneous disintegration of stone and ivy composing the circular dungeon where formerly the prisoner had to content himself with only two small apertures optically fusing into one; while now, with the disappearance of all walls, he can survey the entire circular landscape), or absolute nothingness, *nichto*" (p. 161). The latter alternative is impossible to imagine or visualize, since it is an essentially inhuman state. But the former is one of Nabokov's recurrent theories, combining his speculations about physical death with deliberate creative self-annihilation, a process of artistic creation.

What Krug imagines as "perfect knowledge," or "death," is the shrugging off of a single personality in *Sebastian Knight*, or the "dying" of Shade, and his subsequent fusion with other modes of being and other kinds of psychological "knowledge." The disappearance of the walls of stage scenery in the end of *Invitation to a Beheading*, and the withdrawing of the "wall" in the end of *Bend Sinister*, suggest the widening of vision, the return to the omniscient narrator and a reminder of the deceptive illusion of his narrative. Thus death in some

significant sense occurs only in the mind of the author.
Death is often synonymous with his casting off the guise
of one character in order to assume another (Sebastian's
and Shade's deaths), or with the process of a fictional
character being divested of his temporarily created self,
and subsumed by his creator.

If the author himself directs and contains the characters
in his fiction, and has the power of springing them into
"life" and depriving them of his life, then the statement
at the end of *Bend Sinister*, that Krug had learned "that
death was but a question of style" (p. 222), is consistent
with Krug's earlier discussions. Krug sees that the end
of his life is, in a "circular landscape," curving back to
his childhood, to the school courtyard, and to the main
actors appearing as children. Superimposed on Krug's
version of "reality" is the courtyard, where the main
actors are adults who regard Krug as mad. Beyond this
level of "reality" we are made aware that the yard and
the characters are fictional, and already beginning to give
place to another shade of "reality": Krug "saw the Toad
crouching at the foot of the wall, shaking, dissolving,
speeding up his shrill incantations, protecting his dimming face with his transparent arm" (p. 221). The imaginary world is crumbling, and the political oppressor is
being dissolved by his superior victim, or by the author
who transcends both. Thus "death" is "a question of
style" in the sense that it is a problem of description, of
representation, of conveying an abstract problem in terms
of verbal play and the rotation of images.

Death as an aspect of literary technique, and time as a
part of a fusion of observed patterns, are closely related,
since both theories assume that death and time are
chiefly mental phenomena, and that both can be stylistically captured. On the bridge, the pattern on the para-

pet, the solace of the bas-relief conveys a joy in detail which stops time. A collection of such patterns might have prevented Olga's death. Therefore, "life" is perhaps the intense awareness of conscious contact. The contact itself may be physical or emotional-intellectual, but the perception of a pattern within the contact is necessarily verbal, since the observations can be formulated only through language.

The solace of language, literature, and allusive texture is a crucial contrast to the restrictive horror of Paduk's regime. Indeed, by partly placing Paduk and his reign in a childhood game of Krug's imagination and in a literary context, the novel implies that the thinker is intrinsically independent of political systems. The pattern of literary allusions and discussions is part of the daily life of Krug's world. In his room "Gregoire, a huge stag beetle wrought of pig iron which had been used by his grandfather to pull off by the heel (hungrily gripped by these burnished mandibles) first one riding boot, then the other, peered, unloved, from under the leathern fringe of a leathern armchair" (p. 36). Later, when Krug is composing, "Gregoire peered from under the armchair" (p. 179).

This reference to Kafka's Gregor in "The Metamorphosis" is not simply a "bone offered to Kafka fans looking for a similar temperament in *Bend Sinister*," as Page Stegner claims (p. 82). An awareness of a similarity in setting is jokingly acknowledged. Both the novel and Kafka's story concern dream-plots, the grotesque worked out in realistic detail, the mental agony dramatized as physical action. But whereas the Kafka hero is a helpless and half-willing victim of the nightmare, and his world is entirely bounded and defined by the evil design, Nabokov's character contains and is the dreamer-creator of the sinister bend in his fate; he remains superior to the forces of totalitarianism, and retains his awareness of a brighter, gentler, more passionate mode of being.

In addition to the Shakespeare discussion and allusions, which I will examine at some length, a reflection of a brighter and more passionate realm is glimpsed through the quotations from Catullus ("brevis lux," "da mi basia mille") and Mallarmé ("le sanglot dont j'étais encore ivre"), and through Krug's own beautifully imagined letter of Olga and the hawk-moth (pp. 125–127) and his dream of Olga taking off her jewels after the ball of earthly life (pp. 77–78, a scene containing a fleeting murmur of Maupassant's short story "The Necklace").

The recurring image of the moth is one of delicate, fragile shades and patterns, of aesthetic and emotional solace. There is a print of "an oscellated hawk moth and its shagreen caterpillar" in Quist's shop (p. 166), and a truncated evocation linking Mariette to "the pink moth clinging" (p. 181), which is interrupted by Krug's arrest. Like the puddle which spans the inner and outer fictional circles in *Bend Sinister*, the moth appears in the creative imagination of the hero (Krug's letter), in the world of fictional convention as an object which is part of the setting in a shop (Quist's print), and finally at the omniscient author's window (pp. 221–222), when we are already outside the narrative. The loveliness of the moth is thus a permanent and enduring imprint on all levels of the novel, and acts as another of the several connections between author and main character. (Even Krug's exterior bears the imprint of the moth-pattern in the color and shape of his bow-tie.) Some of the minor characters also briefly take part in acts of artistic assertion, such as the student ball, a dance " 'before an empty house' " (p. 43), and the "waltwhitmanesque" painter who rearranges chronological time to suit his subjective reality (p. 90).

These various images of gaiety, courage, and aesthetic pleasure are fleeting yet powerful contrasts to Paduk's brutal, mindless regime.

The most prominent literary pattern in *Bend Sinister* is formed by the whimsical *Hamlet* discussion between Krug and Ember in Chapter 7. As the author, or Krug, informs us, "There are two themes here: the Shakespearean one rendered in the present tense, with Ember presiding in his ruelle; and another theme altogether, a complex mixture of past, present, and future, with Olga's monstrous absence causing dreadful embarrassment" (p. 101). We are told that Ember is arranging a production of *Hamlet*, trying to use his own translation of the play for the performance, though he is still in the process of finishing his version. Even before the *Hamlet* discussion, Nabokov has some fun with this theme: Ember is attempting to translate "his favorite line in Shakespeare's greatest play——

> follow the perttaunt jauncing 'neath the rack
> with her pale skeins-mate." (P. 34.)

This line is Nabokov's invention, although the words themselves are used separately in various plays of "dze Bart." But Ember is hampered not only by the rival, atrocious translation into which his actors lapse, but also by a ludicrous and sinister political interpretation (in which Fortinbras, or "Ironside," is the main character), and an incongruous, incomplete cast. Thus Ember, the producer within, is duplicated and extended in the character of Krug, the producer-dreamer of the whole plot, and by the omniscient dream-manager who encircles both.

The nightmare *Hamlet* plot of the novel contains fat Krug (Gertrude describes Hamlet in V.ii.274 as "fat and scant of breath"), who absents himself from felicity to tell his own story, and his faithful friend (Ember), who exits before the hero. The father-son relationship is retained, but with the reversal of having the son innocently murdered in a garden which looks like an "open-air theatre" (p. 201). The two spies, pretending to be organ-grinders (p. 115), may be the transposed shadows of Rosencrantz and Guildenstern (labeled "an absurd duality" by Krug). The antique-dealer, Quist, who kisses Krug's shoulder with what appears to be genuine affection, is perhaps the distorted version of Laertes, who is both a friend of Hamlet and in league with Claudius. This debased modern Laertes boasts to Krug about a duel in which he killed a noble opponent who offended his sister by characterizing her as " 'cette petite Phryné qui se croit Ophélie' " (p. 168).

The *agent provocateur's* name may be a pun on "qui est," like Quilty's in *Lolita* ("qui est-il"). Quist is probably the character seen earlier—"Who was that idly sitting on a fence?" (p. 89)—in the country, his role made emblematic by his position as a fence-sitter. Quist alludes to the country scene when Krug did not want to carry David to the station, but he quickly corrects himself before Krug notices (p. 169). Slight Shakespeare ripples also appear in the name of Krug's housekeeper (Claudina) and Olga's relatives: "Viola, Viola's revolting husband, a half brother of sorts" (p. 80).

As L. L. Lee notes, the three portraits in Ember's room "have something to do with the Bacon-Shakespeare nonsense," there are quotations from the Baconian Sir Edwin Durning-Lawrence, the German commentator Horn (in the Ekwilist version of *Hamlet*), and Ruskin and C. Elliot Browne (in the derivation of Ophelia's name).[2] The Shakespeare theme is closely connected with the basic

[2] L. L. Lee, *"Bend Sinister*: Nabokov's Political Dream," in *Nabokov*, ed. L. S. Dembo, pp. 98–103.

outline of *Bend Sinister*. Hamlet, when speaking to
Rosencrantz and Guildenstern, sees his world in entirely
subjective and metaphoric terms, telling them that "Denmark's a prison" (II.ii.239), and exclaiming: "O God, I
could be bounded in a nut-shell, and count myself a king
of infinite space, were it not that I have bad dreams"
(II.ii.249–51). Hamlet's "bad dream" is the "reality" of
Denmark, here represented as evil springing from the
mind of the hero. In the same way, there are suggestions
in *Bend Sinister* that Paduk's country, like the world of
Invitation to a Beheading, is a prison which unsuccessfully attempts to contain the main character. And the
action of *Bend Sinister*, as of *Hamlet*, may be no more
than the dramatization of the "bad dreams" of its hero.
Furthermore—to carry the idea to a typically Nabokovian
level of receding reality—the structure of both works may
consist of the dramatization of the author's metaphors,
which occasionally flower into vivid "lifelike" scenes
and characters, or remain theoretical speculations (as in
Hamlet's soliloquies, and Krug's philosophical writings).

Ember has translated Hamlet's "To be, or not to be"
speech into Russian and French (both are parodic ren-
derings). The doubts expressed in this speech are similar
to Krug's writings on death:

> To be, or not to be, that is the question:
> Whether 'tis nobler in the mind to suffer
> The slings and arrows of outrageous fortune,
> Or to take arms against a sea of troubles,
> And by opposing end them: To die, to sleep,
> No more; and by sleep to say we end
> The heartache, and the thousand natural shocks
> That flesh is heir to? 'Tis a consummation
> Devoutly to be wish'd. To die; to sleep;
> To sleep! perchance to dream! ay, there's the rub;
> For in that sleep of death what dreams may come,
> . . . Must give us pause; . . . the dread of something
>   after death,

The undiscover'd country from whose bourn
No traveler returns, puzzles the will,
And makes us rather bear those ills we have. (III.i.56–81.)

Hamlet's initial "question" can be interpreted (as in
Samuel Johnson's reading in Furness Variorum *Hamlet*,
p. 205) as a speculation about the after-life (as Johnson
paraphrases it, "whether *after our present state, we are
to be, or not to be*"). Krug has wondered whether death
is perfect knowledge or a state of nothingness, and elsewhere Nabokov's characters are tormented by the vision
of after-life as a kind of madness. For Hamlet death is
either pure sleep or sleep teeming with dreams. Johnson
equates dreaming with retaining "our powers of sensibility," and in this sense "bad dreams" after death
would constitute a sensibility tormented by danger and
evil, a description of most of the action of *Bend Sinister*.
Krug's hesitation and indecision about escaping from his
country is due to his inability to believe that the threats
and the political figures are "real," rather than a part of
his own nightmare.

The head of the Ekwilist state, Paduk, is a deliberately
stylized, semi-animated figure. In the ballad which Hamlet recites to Horatio after the play within the play, he
summarizes the political situation in which his father was
replaced by his uncle: "For thou dost know, O Damon
dear, / This realm dismantled was / of Jove himself; and
now reigns here / A very, very-pajock" (III.ii.269–272).
"Pajock" is glossed by Theobald as a "paddock or toad"
(Furness Variorum *Hamlet*, p. 262), and Hamlet likens
Claudius to a "paddock" in his interview with his mother
(III.iv.190). In *Bend Sinister*'s cinematic version of *Hamlet*, one of the early scenes was to present this flash of
the political situation: "A toad breathes and blinks in
the late king's favourite garden seat" (106), perhaps a

visualization of the lines about the "pajock," but at any rate certainly a parallel suggested between the usurpation in *Hamlet* and Paduk's coming to power. Paduk, or The Toad, is a flat, subhuman character, whose nickname serves to emphasize his role as a mere prop in a fable (Krug christens one schoolboy incident with the fairy-tale-like name of "The Kiss of the Toad").

Paduk's unreality is heightened by his deliberate imitation of the external appearance of a cartoon character called "Etermon" (Everyman), who, along with a senile philosopher's theories, was the original inspiration for Ekwilism. But neither the philosopher Skotoma (whose name, L. L. Lee points out, means "murder" in modern Greek), nor Paduk realizes that there is no such thing as "everyman"; beyond the apparent similarity of bleak exteriors, each "Etermon" nourishes a unique passion, or vision. As the omniscient author intervenes to assert: "The average vessels are not as simple as they appear: it is a conjuror's set and nobody, not even the enchanter himself, really knows what and how much they hold" (p. 75). This insight differentiates the artist's sensibility from that of the political theorist or the revolutionary-turned-tyrant; the discovery of the private and unique qualities of every being is a marvel and mystery even to the author who manipulates them. Paduk the tyrant combines the sartorial aspects of Etermon with the image of a heartless assassin: "a sort of cartoon angularity, a cracked and soiled cellophane wrapper effect, through which, nevertheless, one could discern a brand-new thumbscrew, a bit of rope, a rusty knife, and a specimen of the most sensitive of human organs wrenched out together with its blood-clotted roots" (p. 76). Paduk is both evil and yet without substance, a sinister puppet who is robot-like and emotionless, as are his political

henchmen. When Paduk's role becomes transparent, he
is transformed into the actor beneath the part (as in the
interview, the prison scene, and the final courtyard scene).

In addition to the *Hamlet* reflection, *Bend Sinister* explores and parodies various other religious and literary
motifs. There are numerous allusions to "the fall": the
hero's first name is Adam, Dr. Alexander is described as
"a very Satan of persuasiveness" (p. 45), and references
to apples recur frequently. For instance, the daughter of
the university president, who is tempting Adam into academic safety, shows her father a bowl of apples, later
served to the faculty (pp. 43, 44), and the spy for the
evil political order "hawked apples" (p. 149; cf. also pp.
15, 203, 206).

The maid Mariette is an amalgam of numerous allusive
hints. She is a scrawny Eve who posed naked in her previous "place" before the revolution; she is in contact
with enemy spies who have sent her to seduce Adam;
and Krug asks himself whether she is his daughter. A
rudimentary Mariette first appears on Krug's porch as a
"sketchy little Carmen" (p. 58), kissing a boy dressed as
an "American Football Player" after a masked ball. When
she applies for the maid's job, Krug recalls seeing her,
"probably on the stairs" (p. 128); later he finds in her
room a "Spanish fan and a pair of castanets," as well as
a rose (p. 147). Her late return from the ball also reminds
Krug of Cinderella (pp. 129, 147, 191), whose sisters are
enjoying an active social life, and who is carried down
Krug's staircase, losing a slipper. In describing these slippers, Krug observes that Mariette's were "old bed
slippers trimmed with dirty fur" (p. 147). This is an
ironic distortion of Cinderella's dainty dancing slippers,
and a probable allusion to the mistake which any punning
translator would delight in, where the French Cinderella's
fur slipper (*pantoufle en vair*) was mistranslated into glass

slipper (*en verre*) in English. Mariette is also briefly linked to the Mallarmé line from "The Afternoon of a Faun," "le sanglot dont j'étais encore ivre" (p. 77). When Krug inspects her room he finds a perfume called Sanglot.

Several of these strands connected with Mariette are brought together when Krug reflects on how she spends her time: "She had two *afternoons* off, probably full of *fauns* and *footballers* and *matadors*. . . . Who is she— a servant? an *adopted child*?" (p. 150, my italics). Mariette is a striking but characteristic creation, assembled through the associative faculty of Krug. Her figure is gradually sketched into the first blurry outline on the doorstep, and she combines the texture of fairytales, Catullus, Mallarmé, Mérimée (two "real" names which sound like distortions of each other), and a sinister Ophelia-Eve. Her portrait is constantly in the process of being turned inside out so that her actions correspond to unexpected details in the allusive fabric which gives her a semblance of personality.

Through the interpenetration of imaginative imprints —of moths, puddles, literary references, and cross-references within the novel—the book gives shape to the joint creative consciousness of main character and author. This joint consciousness builds up and then tears down the illusion of a specific place and time, thereby demonstrating the transcendent value of emotional awareness and literary technique. Time and space are aspects of artistic landscapes, boundaries deliberately created to define the nightmares and pleasures of existence.

Krug's death is the dissolution of the fictional wall which separated him from his creator: "And the wall vanished, like a rapidly withdrawn slide, and I stretched myself and got up from among the chaos of written and rewritten pages" (p. 221). The images of Krug's life and thoughts have been projected for us on the screen of

the written page, through changing scenes giving the illusion of depth and development. The omniscient author
reflects that the life of the plot had been a mere "play
upon words" (p. 222). The final reappearance of the
puddle and the moth reasserts the primacy of shape and
pattern combined with the game-like hunt as the metaphors for novelistic creation. The mad Krug re-imagines
Olga's and David's deaths as part of "some silly theatri-
cals, she getting drowned, he losing his life or something
in a railway accident" (p. 218). Krug's death, in turn, is
placed within a theatrical, deliberately ludicrous and disjointed courtyard scene, in which he plays the madman
and the Fool. The simultaneous pathos and distancing
which results from this change of role prepares the reader
for Krug's dissolution into the authorial "I" whose consciousness completes the circle of patterned details.

VII

ADA
The Spiral Texture of
Details, Doubles, and Artistry

A MEMOIR, a sexual Bildungsroman, a philosophical novel, a "family romance," and a "talking palette," *Ada* mimics numerous genres and conventions. With its parodies and allusions, *Ada*, like Nabokov's previous novels, reaches out to the process of creation, to the series of acts, parodies, experiences, metaphors, and perceptions which emerge from the imagination in a subjective temporal sequence and which the author's craft assembles into a whole. The materials of Nabokov's artistic creation are, first, the search for the realm of "curiosity, tenderness, kindness, ecstasy"; then the texture of the world created in the process of this search; and over all, the quality of the imaginative perception which animates these materials.

As Van looks toward Ada and his love for her, he creates a fantasy world of passion where their feelings for each other are mirrored onto imagined landscapes.

The shifting topography of this fantasy world includes slides from English, French, and Russian novels, Italian and Dutch painters, and Nabokov's previous novels. The unfolding of the details of this fantasy world shapes *Ada*. The novel's structure lies in the spiral arrangement of details, enriched by allusions to literature and painting, repeated distortedly (hence becoming a source of private allusion), and endowed with meticulously textured "reality." The details spiral toward the author who assembled them with such precision and sense of play, thereby asserting the triumph of artistry over time. The "meaning" of *Ada* lies in the stream and juxtaposition of details which create a unique, artificial world, static moments of felt Time, and imaginative Space. *Ada* thus chronicles not only a manner of artistic creation (allusive, detailed, refracted with discrete mosaics), but also the pleasure and necessity of individual, sensuous perception, as well as the salvation of pattern and design from the horror of loss and death.

In *Ada* the analogy between the intensity of lust and of artistic perception is even more specifically emphasized than in *Lolita*: "It would not be sufficient to say that in his love-making with Ada he discovered the pang, the '*ogon*', the agony of supreme 'reality.' Reality, better say, lost the quotes it wore like claws" (pp. 219–220). (Lucette's and Ada's love-making is described as "anagrams" [p. 375]). Love-making creates an isolated, private awareness which is a form of imaginative creation, and Van's description of the nature of his lust and love-making shapes the structure of *Ada*'s particular reality, a reality built on constant reversals and occasional dark shadows. (The string of brothels in *Ada* is a multiple reflection of detached, loveless sexual encounters which magnify the elements of disease, revulsion, and aimlessness hinted at in Van's and Ada's love. The brothels, like Quilty, form a parodic, sinister double of the main love affair.) Repeated mention is made of Van's sexual sterility, while his artistic labors are described as pregnancies. Van the artist deliberately wrenches himself out of normal roles and expected results: his obsessive, excessive, and solipsistic sexuality is a metaphor for his art, while his sterility may be a hint of the inimitable nature of that art.

Ada expands and combines the theme of time as explored in *Bend Sinister* and the theme of artistry-as-lust exemplified in a perverted way by Humbert. Just as Krug both experiences and records his life through an inward, intermittent, and unpredictable mental chronology, Van Veen is simultaneously author and main character of his chronicle. As Humbert's relation to Lolita is a flawed artist's treatment of his subject, so Van's love for Ada is the means by which the artist experiences and creates a unique and absorbing subjective reality. *Ada*, like *Bend Sinister*, repeatedly underlines its structural and stylistic concern with the philosophy of time, especially in Van's chronic speculations.

Ada herself is a kind of mirror of literary associations (particularly with Byron, whose physical prowess is reflected in Van's Mascodagama stunt and *byronka* or "open shirt," and whose sexual fantasies are literalized in Van's amours) and of Van's lust for originality of style. Her name is a mirror name (the same read backwards as forwards—an idea Humbert says he toyed with in *Lolita*). Ada is a creation of Van, but also—like Lolita —a creation which frequently eludes and tortures its creator. Her identity is formed by the patterns of details which affect Van. Her character exists only insofar as Van recollects and recreates his feelings towards her: "The rapture of her identity . . . shows a complex system of those subtle bridges which the senses traverse—laughing, embraced, throwing flowers in the air—between membrane and brain, which always was and is a form of memory, even at the moment of its perception" (pp. 220–221).[1]

In *Ada* the "texture of time" is the texture of human consciousness recording itself, hence the texture of prose style. This literary and stylistic exploration of time is presented through intermittently animated metaphors which constantly move backward and forward between vividly visualized and philosophical scenes. The texture of time is the rich awareness of physical, intellectual, and emotional projections on the imaginative surface of Van's remembrance. This remembrance is set into the joint perspective of Van's theories and speculations about time, and into novelistic and painterly parodies and allusions. These frames of reference serve as illuminating thematic and metaphoric connections within the structure of the novel, pointing to the creative imagination of its author.

Ada expands and literalizes the theme of the writer's lifelong torrid affair with language and with maddeningly enticing images. This affair is incestuous because both the imagination and its verbal approximations, resulting in visualized flashes, spring from the same creative source. *Ada* is a novel not only about the artist and about writing novels, but also about the nature and role of literary conventions and prose style. The quality and characteristics of "that originality of literary style which constitutes the only real honesty of a writer" (p. 471) is the main subject, which subsumes the exploration of the texture of time and passion. The anguish, arrogance, deg-

[1] This is an image of the concept described in Humbert Humbert's article on "Mimir and Memory": "A theory of perceptual time based on the circulation of the blood and conceptually depending . . . on the mind's being conscious not only of matter but also of its own self, thus creating a continuous spanning of two points (the storable future and the stored past)" (*Lolita*, p. 237).

radation, and occasional brutality which vie in promi-
nence with gaiety, scintillation, glamour, and lust in the
novel are ways of approximating the artistic agony of
trying to create wisps of flesh and blood on a printed
page. As the novel's subtitle indicates, time is treated in
terms of literary and stylistic progression within the
genre of the "family chronicle." As Robert Alter notes
in his essay on *Ada*, the novel is "a parodistic review of
the development of the novel,"[2] or, in Alfred Appel's
words, "a museum of the novel."[3]

The theme of the development of the novel genre is not
only parodied but also inverted and internalized within
Ada in order to emphasize the nature of time as subjective, literary, and artistically controllable. The theme is
woven into the plot of *Ada* to create a feeling of time as
part of the particular "reality" of imagined, parodied, or
remembered literary scenes. *Ada* is Nabokov's *Orlando*
(and much, much more) in that it presents a group of
characters who act out a fictionalized charade of imagina-
tive-erotic maturation within a retrospective and highly
allusive chronicle.

In Chapter 15 Van and Ada are still only keeping diaries, a kind of self-directed precursor to the novel, which
corresponds sexually to Van's masturbatory phase. The
ending of the chapter parodies the novelistic convention
of staging coincidences to bring lovers together. Van and
Ada rush back to the house at the same time in order to
hide their diaries: "Then Van and Ada met in the passage,
and would have kissed at some earlier stage of the Novel's
Evolution in the History of Literature. It might have been
a neat little sequel to the Shattal Tree incident. Instead,

[2] Robert Alter, "Nabokov's Ardor," *Commentary*, XLVIII (August, 1969), 48.
[3] Alfred Appel, Jr., "*Ada* Described," *Tri-Quarterly*, XVII
(Winter, 1970), 161.

both resumed their separate ways—and Blanche, I suppose, went to weep in her bower" (p. 96). The "passage"
could be either a corridor of the house or a part of a literary text. The meeting is teasingly suggested and the
reader's expectation is sketched in. But the clumsy use
of coincidence belongs to earlier examples of the genre,
and the author sidesteps the facile solution.

Blanche is presented here as the embodiment of the
disappointed sentimental reader. Blanche, like Mariette
of *Bend Sinister*, is an amalgam of Cendrillon, the available servant girl, the adoring and despairing lower-class
girl in love with the young master, and even as Ada's
shadowy double (p. 398). In the scene when she confesses
her love to Van, her language is "elegiac and stilted, as
spoken only in obsolete novels" (p. 292). Van and Ada's
initial flirtation is described through an analogy with the
stylistic awkwardness of old-fashioned romantic tales:
"The vague commonplaces of vague modesty so dreadful-
ly in vogue eighty years ago, the unsufferable banalities
of shy wooing buried in old romances as arch as Arcady,
those moods, those modes, lurked no doubt behind the
hush of his ambuscades, and that of her toleration" (pp.
98–99). Nabokov's parody of the traditional novel here
takes the involuted form of having the structure of his
plot mimic stilted style. Striking and exaggerated plot
movements are often used as reflections and comic lit-
eralizations of conventional absurdities of phrasing or
characterization.

The persistent return of the novel to metaphor emphasizes the nature of its prose style. Ada says about time:
"It is like——" (p. 563), and with this statement ends a
major section of the book. Concepts can only be expressed
through verbal novelties; the interest lies not in the originality of the idea but in the startling phrasing or unique
apprehension of it, which lends ideas a new and personal

life. *Ada* is the "realization" of a family chronicle in the sense that the novel defines the verb: "to possess the reality of a fact by forcing it into the sensuous center" (p. 251). This act of realization is a feat of the imagination through the medium of prose style.

The striking nature of the metaphor may lie in its combination of images, colors and details, manifesting the "individual vagaries" (p. 237) which characterize art and genius for Nabokov. Shifting emotions, receding levels of reality, distorted temporal sequences shape the chronicle of artistic creation and its emotional landscape in *Ada*. The novel challenges and repudiates the concept of time as relentless progression. Its action moves by means of intense feeling and sensuous thought, which occasionally flower into densely "realized" scenes. Language creates furrows in fictional space where time stands still or whirls around the lovingly constructed prose surface; the duration and intensity of time is portrayed through scenes of sensuality. These scenes form a remembered pattern of details and emotions, a sensual-literary landscape. The elaborately wrought artificial landscape, and the telescoping of historical events, languages, and races, deliberately stress the fictional quality of the world of the novel. Terra and Anti-Terra are distorted reflections of each other and of the "real" world.

Most of *Ada* takes place on Anti-Terra, an imaginary time-space, while Terra is described as either a philosophical hypothesis or an insane projection. The Terra–Anti-Terra division has a dual significance. For Nabokov the "real" world is more distant and inconceivable than an imagined interior one. "Reality" only exists in our perceptions and self-realizations, it is a distorted, subjectively apprehended anti-world. The novel's cosmology and geography toy with various "realized" ideas about the imagination, though we are ultimately reminded that we have been reading a fictional work which dissolves into the world of Terra. This final shift transfers the characters into the "reality" of the reader's imaginative world. Terra and Anti-Terra can also be interpreted as the delineations of two kinds of perception: a mad, unearthly, jumbled consciousness of the relationship of words to objects and feelings, and a more literalistic, more easily recognizable and assimilable portrayal of the human consciousness in the everyday world. Like the landscape of Zembla and New Wye in *Pale Fire*, these two worlds form the internal geography of the realm of art.

In *Ada* the nature of prose style is largely explored through parody (specific allusions, stylistic echoes, and structural imitations of other writers), as well as through an attempt to approximate the effect of paintings through prose. The pictorial details and descriptions of actual and imagined paintings are numerous and dazzling in *Ada*, and these descriptions flesh out the dimension of prose as concrete and sensual. The shrubbery and statuary in the brothel scenes are taken from the conventional English novel, but become the setting for the theme of lust and sexual indulgence so carefully masked by the civilized amenities of the genre—as practiced by Jane Austen, for example. *Ada*'s texture of allusions and puns combines painterly and literary images in order to suggest a mode of artistic perception. Just as Ada's film, "Don Juan's Last Fling," crosses the figures of Don Juan and Don Quixote, Van is made to mirror the self-indulgence, Romantic conventionality, and brutal sensuality of Don Juan, as well as Don Quixote's awareness of hopelessness, death, finality, and dignity of proud gesture. Thus *Ada* collapses Time and Space by making them into an artificially "real" Time-Space. Death and loss are transformed into processes of human perception, and become parts of patterns which are assimilable, comprehensible, felt. This seems to be the author's special intention in *Ada*, and I like its manors.

2

The hero-narrator and the omniscient author are achingly aware of the struggle of a live consciousness juggling the empty categories of time and lust into patterned and evocative details of intense duration of felt love. Ada, in the capacity of muse and subject who reveals and embodies artistic reality for the author, generates both ecstasy and suffering. Her unfaithfulness results in the agony, near-madness, loss, and longing which is a necessary component of the Nabokovian vision of artistic creation. Throughout *Ada* the predominantly joyous surface is shot through with jealousy, pain, and the premonition of death. (The editor's initial note that "With the exception of Mr. and Mrs. Ronald Oranger, a few incidental figures, and some non-American citizens, all the persons mentioned by name in this book are dead," provides a chilling and essentially distancing perspective. This note forces the reader to regard the characters as "dead souls" from the beginning, and to savor their lifelikeness as an act of stylistic resurrection. Of course, we can always suspect that the rubric of "incidental figures," by a trick of semantic relativism, includes Van and Ada, if we consider metaphors as the main "figures" of the novel.)

Van promises Ada that he will "redeem" their childhood by writing the book we are reading (p. 406), just as Marcel toward the end of *Remembrance of Things Past* is ready to begin writing the novel we are just finishing. Ada's "tumescence of retrieved time" is an echo and triumphant reversal of the title of Proust's masterpiece. Swann and his "cattleya" are alluded to (p. 56) as a reminder of tormenting sexual obsession, and we are warned to beware the "marcel wave of fashionable art," "the Proustian bed and the assassin pun" (p. 541).

Ada's network of allusions includes not only references to other writers, but also cross-references to some of Nabokov's other novels: a weaving in of "Spring in Fialta" (p. 477) and a line of its French song (p. 483); the "muscat" pun from *Pale Fire* (p. 271); the black mask Van shares with V. of *Sebastian Knight* (p. 401). Ada wears a "lolita" to her birthday party and appears as Dolores-Lolita in a film. A novel titled *The Gitanilla* is frequently glimpsed in *Ada*; Lolita is at one point described as "the gitanilla" (*Lolita*, p. 222). Demon might derive his name from Poe's "The Raven." ("Raven" is Demon's alternate nickname, and Lenore appears as Marina's stage name and as the name of an actress who resembles Ada. De Vere of Poe's "Lenore" is also alluded to.) The mention of "Pale Fire with Tom Cox Up" (p. 477), the simulated heart attack on the lectern (p. 548), and the quotation from John Shade (pp. 585–586) allude to *Pale Fire*; during Van's last visit to the last Villa Venus (pp. 356–358) various details reflect back to *Bend Sinister*, such as the ambiguous identity of the adolescent prostitute, recalling Mariette, and the "church clock, never audible except at night," like the clock which strikes twice at the end of *Bend Sinister* (p. 222). (The visit to the floramor is later described by Van as "the purest *sanglot* in the book" [p. 584] recalling the perfume and one of the motifs of *Bend Sinister*.)[4]

[4] In addition to metaphysical and Symbolist poetry, the novel contains several half-concealed allusions to Romantic poetry, such as the echo of Wordsworth's description of Lucy in the vision

The constant shifting of allusions and parodic gears makes fun of the reader's expectations: *Ada* is neither "realistic" nor a pure fantasy, it takes place neither on a recognizably "realistic" earth nor on a completely imagined one (hence the mixture of languages, races, means of locomotion). The main character and author, Van Veen, is a pastiche of traditional fictional heroes: he is a poseur whose exaggerated pride, cynicism, dash, wealth, and potency reflect the *données* of the libertine, but he is also a dreamer and a thinker. Van's love for Ada combines the reciprocated, joyous bliss of John Shade and Sybil with the tormented agony of Kinbote and Disa. (This duality is described as the bright and "shade" side of Van's love, echoing Kinbote's agony [p. 188].) This combination of joy and torment is also reflected in the rapidly changing slides of the different scenes, in the Terra–Anti-Terra division, and in the sinister Demon with angel's wings.

The mirroring and interior reflections within *Ada* are a recurrent method of structuring. This mirroring is manifested in the placing of characters and scenes; it emphasizes the artificial nature of the plot, and reflects gleefully the symmetries and contrasts of traditional novels. The mirroring is evident from the beginning of *Ada*: the twins Aqua and Marina each marry a Walter D. Veen, one nicknamed Raven or Demon Veen and the other Red Veen, born in the same year, suggesting color print duplication. When Ada explains her dilemma to Van in terms of what she calls a "parable" of a girl entangled with three men (p. 192), her parable is repeated

---

of Ada as "gouts and glooms of the woodland passed across her book, her face" (p. 280). Nabokov's use of specific literary allusions is the subject of Simon Karlinsky's illuminating "Nabokov's Russian Games," *New York Times Book Review*, April 18, 1971.

in the plot of the film version of *Les Enfants Maudits*. Marina (who is playing the female lead) objects that she sounds "a hundred years old on this page and fifteen on the next," and that if the film is a flashback the brother-lover "should not know what he seems to know." The director Vronsky replies that " 'it's only a half-hearted flashback' " (p. 201).

As Marina in the film, so Van in the novel is constantly switching between his adolescence and his eighties and nineties, thereby providing us with a time dimension which looks backwards and forwards at the same time that it is describing a present event. Marina's "screen-corrupted mind" retroactively transforms her former passion for Demon into a later film hit of hers, *A Torrid Affair* (p. 253). This is a reversal of Van's process of recreating and imaginatively reliving his love for Ada. Marina's "stale melodrama" is a fitting of emotional experience into hackneyed conventional forms, while Van uses convention to serve as a parodic foil to the unique experience. Marina's inability to "realize" her affair is contrasted to Van's imagination: he has already recreated her affair in the beginning of the novel. But, of course, Marina is only one of Van's puppets, "a dummy in human disguise" without "magically detailed imagination" (p. 252).

Without details the past merges into the present and future in a meaningless, uninterrupted vagueness. It is the re-imagining and reshaping of events which recreates emotion through the shock of novelty in a familiar situation. Van's loving recollection and the author's arrangement and structuring through details suggest parallel fictional lives, symmetrical fates, the acts of a mind playing with ideas and making them into images. Van's description of his novella on the Texture of Time (pp. 562–563) mirrors the technique and summarizes the structure of *Ada*; this interior reflection, like the "blurb," serves to reinforce the hints of artistic control and of the artificial nature of the novel. The compressed description of Nabokov's technique ("illustrative metaphors gradually increasing, very gradually building up to a logical love story, going from past to present, blossoming as a concrete story, and just as gradually reversing analogies and disintegrating again into bland abstraction") illuminates and distances the novel we are reading. Van's novella, like Shade's *Poems* and Sebastian's novels, is a symmetrical detail in the receding reality of the total work, a miniature reflection.

Besides Van's writing, there are minor mirrors of artistry in the novel, especially Mlle. Larivière, Ada's paintings of plants and insects, Kim's photography, the elderly painter who liked little girls, and even the art of cheating at cards. All of the artist figures practice acts of metamorphosis, which result in new combinations of details, producing unexpected images. There are fleeting parodic representations of the artist as Joyce, Proust, Tolstoy, Pushkin, and these representations are approached through Nabokovian distortions—so that the mirror reflects back to the prose style of *Ada* itself. The details of allusions are woven into Van's consciousness, and become a part of his philosophy of time: past authors exist in the present through assimilation and imitation, surrounding the present work with asymmetrical versions of itself.

Repeated scenes within *Ada* are often twisted and parodic—as Van muses when he holds Lucette in his lap in a scene which reminds him of riding home with Ada a few years before: "a set of coincidences slightly displaced; the artistry of asymmetry" (p. 280). Slightly displaced symmetry has the effect of teasing the reader into recalling the earlier scene or detail, it creates a web

of allusions within the novel, and it underlines the idea of
time as a tool of the memory. Van "relives" his earlier
ride with Ada, and the earlier picnic. Lucette, who has a
mosquito bite like Ada's four years before, reminds Van
of "Ada's soft haunches which he now held as if she
were present in duplicate, in two different color prints"
(p. 280). The image of photographic duplication recurs
during Lucette's final boat ride where one of the women
with dark skin and blond hair is a "grotesque caricature"
in photographic terms, the "coarse negative" of Ada (p.
482). During the same boat ride Lucette tells Van that
his shadowy "twin" was present at Ada's wedding, and
Van recalls dreaming about attending the ceremony
which he in fact avoided.

Asymmetrical shadows of the main characters are
placed throughout *Ada*: besides the usher at the wedding,
Van is reflected in Greg (p. 455) and mistaken for "Vivian
Vale" (a name reminiscent of Vivian Darkbloom) by
Ada's "coarse negative" double (p. 483). Ada is imagined
by Van as "twinned" into Cordula, who in turn resembles "his first whorelet" (p. 168). Lucette tells Van
of Ada's affair with a young star named Johnny, "practically her twin in appearance, born the same year, the
same day, the same instant" (p. 380). The recurring "Lenore Collin" is part of Marina's stage name, as well as
an actress who resembles Ada (p. 465). The distorted
repetition of detail and character creates a feeling of
simultaneous control and disjunction. Like the rents and
puddles in the earlier novels, the displaced symmetries
reveal the hand of the artist and the essential "oneness"
(or Van-ness, cf. p. 360) of all the characters and details.
The spatial arrangement teases the reader into making
the connections among details which the author has
scattered.

Nabokov's use of the double is closely related to the

view of fictional characters as mysterious and often sinister projections of the author's process of self-creation. If art is regarded as primarily the representation of a unique sensibility rather than as the recreation of external reality, then artistic creation is a kind of mirroring or doubling of the author's inner self onto the aesthetic plane. The puddles, lakes, mirrors, and windowpanes are media through which the doubling takes place. The rents in the fictional fabric can open Janus-like in opposite directions: inward toward the artist, and outward toward the realm of art. (This process is elaborately illustrated in *Pale Fire*.) The doubling and reflection usually implies a proliferation of personalities and experiences which proceed from the mind of the artist. The mirror-like presentation is an appropriate symbol of the technique of characterization: fictional personae acquire their personalities from details projected by the author onto a shimmering surface which looks toward the reader.

In psychological terms the double is a conventional image of a hidden self which is tantalizingly glimpsed through a chance reflection. The double can also represent a self which is deliberately detached from the material world, a self which can be contemplated from an aesthetic distance. To the madman (who is frequently synonymous with the artist), the double seen in a mirror or lake can represent his "real" self from which his emotional and artistic control separates him (as in *The Eye* or in the relationship between Humbert and Quilty). Death or madness in Nabokov is often seen as a transitional state, or a state where the artistic process operates. Both death and madness allow a transformation and a reimagination of existence. The double may be the repressed self, the devil, the pervert, the assassin, all contained within the negative capability of the artist. The mirror world is a rival to the empirical world, since, paradoxi-

cally, it is more stable and fixed than empirical experience. In a sinister way the mirror world can acquire a
reality of its own, or a reality which obliterates its rival.
Death often comes when there is an attempt to merge
with the double. This attempt shatters the protective
shell of a single personality and can lead either to self-
annihilation or to a multiplication of the self into diverse
imaginative creations. The mirroring and doubling reflect back to the controlling patterns of the artist within
or behind the narrative.

In *Ada*, scenes, motifs, lines are often complete in
themselves, or in the pattern of repetitions and distortions
in which they occur. (For instance, the phrase "Destroy
and forget," the antithesis of Van's artistry, which is
used several times in various contexts [pp. 290, 397,
421] to remind us of the author's imprint behind Van's
narrative, or the recurring fur slipper snatched from
Bend Sinister and seen by the drowning Lucette.) The
fictional illusion is more consistently and gleefully punc-
tured in *Ada* than in any previous Nabokov novel, at
the same time that there is a proportional intensity of
"realistic" detail. The cinematic, novelistic, and dramatic instructions to the characters are coupled with
directions to the reader about how to interpret and ap-
preciate the novel. Young Ada's interest in collecting,
painting, and combining the qualities of various species
of flowers and insects is fitted into the theme of art by
the explanation that "reality and natural science are
synonymous in the terms of this, and only this, dream"
(p. 77). Her passionate absorption in the arrangement
and imaginative juxtaposition of a scientific discipline is
a reflection of Van's depiction of ideas of love and time
through prose images. We are also directed toward the
web of details by Van who tells us that "the microscope
of reality" is "the only reality" (p. 221), and Ada insists

that we should focus "on the subjective and unique poetry of the author" (p. 426).

The cast of characters is rendered deliberately fictional and patterned to the careful reader: Marina, Dan, and Demon share the same birthday, just as Shade, Kinbote, and Gradus had; Aqua wears yellow slacks and a black bolero for her picnic-suicide (p. 28), as does Ada on the day Van leaves her after finding out about her infidelity (p. 295), and Lucette puts on black slacks and a lemon shirt for her suicide (p. 492). The sharing of moles, parents, birthdays, outfits, and phrases is the author's hint that the characters are manipulated, and that they are aspects of a single creative consciousness. The disjunctive patterns form the connecting web of the unique reality of the novel.

The narrator criticizes Ada's governess, Mlle. Laparure (or Larivière), for her version of Maupassant's *La Rivière de Diamants*: "The story lacked 'realism' *within its own terms*, since a punctilious, penny-counting employee would have found out, first of all . . . what exactly the lost necklace had cost" (p. 87). Every work should create its own "reality"; even a story with a fixed, conventional subject should at least be consistent. The hackneyed theme of social classes requires precise details to be credible. In sharp contrast to Mlle. Larivière's banal plots (her work is always described in terms of its action rather than its style or details), *Ada* provides the reader with no fixed terms or *données*. Its main interest, as of Nabokov's other novels, is in the pattern and shimmer of details. As Van informs us, "detail is all" (p. 60).

It is an unsettling experience for most readers that these patterns of details do not tend toward a single, unified, fictional world, nor toward a central web other than the author himself. Rather, the elements of Nabokov's novels remain discrete mosaics which alternately illuminate different aspects of the themes and characters. Instead of contributing to the fleshing out of a character or subject, the details often form unrelated blocks in the airy buildings of the novels. Such blocks serve to emphasize the breathtaking gaps and leaps of the imagination manifesting itself in artistic creation. The aesthetic pleasure of contemplating a pattern of details rivals and surpasses the interest of conventional plot and character development. Instead of a continuous fictional landscape we are left with flashes of verbal wit and emotional insight whose very discontinuities underline the mystery of human consciousness and the struggle to present this mystery. Discontinuities, disillusionments, detailed images, glimpses of the author, imaginative leaps, and shifting genres are the terms consistently observed.

Nabokov's style implicitly deprecates logic and rationality; the reader is constantly made uneasy by being deluded into an illusory density of realistic details, and then suddenly told that the detail is part of an artificially staged, opaque scene. Frequently the fiction fades away, leaving only the author's grin behind. The patterning of Nabokov's novels is a kind of discipline and a game; the pattern deliberately undermines the lifelikeness of the plot and reminds us of the author's control, as well as of the delights of language and verbal mosaics. Nabokov's style aims to give a sense of the world as a sensual experience, as a series of impressions coalescing in patches of vivid scenes, only to dissolve in further images. The pattern often consists of repeated details or images (such as the puddle in *Bend Sinister*) which are similar but slightly distorted, as if viewed through a vibrating kaleidoscope. The distortion of repeated images sometimes serves to emphasize the plot movement between different levels of reality: the fictional surroundings of the main character, his fantasy life, and the omniscient author encircling both. Empirical experience is shown to possess no solidity, and even the mind and the imagination are a shifting, mysterious quicksand of images and impressions. Instead of a consistent fictional illusion we are presented with a series of illuminations and images which verbally approximate the experience of intense, fleeting sensation, and the human consciousness absorbing this sensation.

3

In his fiction as well as in his memoirs, Nabokov eschews the smoothly oiled fitting of objects into symbolically contrived situations. His insistently discontinuous yet patterned details suggest that all we can observe are fleeting shapes and seeming symbols whose appropriateness is fragile and momentary. The conscious patterning does not falsify because it does not pretend to imitate empirical experience. The reaction of the beholder creates a unique, subjective pattern. In *Speak, Memory*, Nabokov recalls a visit to his retired and pathetic governess, and afterwards sees an old swan awkwardly and unsuccessfully trying to lift itself into a boat: It "all seemed for a moment laden with that strange significance which sometimes in dreams is attached to a finger pressed to mute lips and then pointed at something the dreamer has no time to distinguish before waking with a start" (pp. 77–78).

The "strange significance" glimpsed through the pathos of the swan springs from the emotional state of the perceiver. The reaction to the swan's "symbolic" struggle places the governess and the swan in an artistic pattern. Nabokov's fiction circles around moments of elusive emotional significance. His style attempts to capture the quality of elusiveness through weaving a discontinuous fabric whose designs metaphorically suggest the relation between emotion and perception. Logical discourse and conventional plot and narration are constantly broken off, to be replaced by the vividness of subjective reaction and private patterns. These breaks produce the sensation of observing fleeting reality through the author's controlling consciousness. The "fleeting" impression is created by juxtaposing symbolic object and emotional reaction against the background of conventional narration.

The struggle between reader and author (which represents the main action of a work of art from an affective point of view) aims to force the reader into a realm of perception where ready-made literary assumptions dissolve into the author's variations on the illusion of reality. Van's dramatized "notes" "on the general character of dreams" (pp. 362–364) is a discourse on symbolism in a playfully imagined classroom setting. Van explains to a rather slow audience that the terms of a comparison are both "real, concrete, existing things. . . . Neither is a symbol of the other . . . ; they are not interchangeable, not tokens of something else." When Van is about to meet Ada after a long separation, he sees that "a dead and dry hummingbird moth lay on the window ledge of the lavatory. Thank goodness, symbols did not exist either in dreams or the life in between" (p. 510).

The moth, like the swan in *Speak, Memory*, is a specific, melancholy object in itself, and its juxtaposition with Van's emotional state serves to heighten the vividness of both, as well as to suggest the imprint of the author. The moth is a part of the butterfly design of the novel, just as the naked, bandaged doll Dan gives Ada on her birthday (p. 84) recalls Aqua's stillborn child and is part of the pattern of the "foetus"-like rubber doll Lucette floats in water, which in turn distortedly mirrors her suicide. The refusal to construct symbolic images and the insistence on the concrete specificity of objects assert the primacy of detail over meaning. In fact, meaning is thus defined as the juxtaposition of metaphoric terms and the aesthetic pleasure which attends the perception of a particular design.

Ada forces us to regard the details of the work in process as primary. The monstrous, agonizing, and often trivial incidents which create moments of pure "realization" are stressed as discrete episodes. When Demon watches Marina's talentless performance in a hackneyed play, he creates his own moment of revelation as he sees her running into the orchard: "Her meeting with Baron O., who strolled out of a side alley, all spurs and green tails, somehow eluded Demon's consciousness, so struck was he by the wonder of that brief abyss of absolute reality between two bogus fulgurations of fabricated life" (p. 12). The echoes of this scene resonate through the narrative of *Ada*: the Baron O. of the play is the shadow of Baron d'O., or d'Onsky, who is Marina's lover outside the play.

The unfolding of Demon's discovery of Marina's unfaithfulness is a teasing example of the interpenetration of various levels of "action" within *Ada*. Demon, at a meal with the "art expert" Baron d'Onsky, shows his companion a small painting he believes to be "an unknown product of Parmigianino's tender art" (p. 12). It portrays a naked girl holding an apple, and recalls Marina, "when, rung out of a hotel bathroom by the phone, . . . muffled the receiver while asking her lover something that he could not make out because the bath's voice drowned her whisper" (p. 13). Demon assures d'Onsky that the two of them "were the sole people to have admired it *en connaissance de cause*" (p. 13), and the resemblance to Marina is not mentioned between the two men. But a garrulous female visitor of Demon's the

next day, upon seeing Marina, remarks on her resemblance to " 'Eve on the Clepsydrophone' in Parmigianino's famous picture," eliciting Demon's observation
that the picture is not famous and she can't have seen it
(p. 14). Demon then challenges and wounds d'Onsky at
a duel, and writes in a farewell letter to Marina: "One
image I shall not forget and will not forgive. . . . I rang
you up at your hotel room. . . , you said you were in Eve's
state, hold the line, let me put on a *penyuar*. Instead,
blocking my ear, you spoke, I suppose, to the man with
whom you had spent the night. . . . Now *that* is the sketch
made by a young artist in Parma, in the sixteenth century,
for the fresco of *our* destiny, in a prophetic trance, and
coinciding, except for the apple of terrible knowledge,
with an image repeated in two men's minds" (p. 16).

The disjointed symmetry of this incident is characteristically Nabokovian: d'Onsky's recognition of the resemblance of the painting to Marina is definitive proof
for Demon that d'Onsky is her lover. The scene in the
hotel bedroom is initially described with Demon as the
lover who shares the room with her, but in Demon's letter the role is replaced by d'Onsky. The origin or prototype of this scene is Parmigianino's painting, stressing
the idea of earlier art as a source for parody (telephone
substituted for apple, "Clepsydrophone" as a comic foreshadowing of the words dorophone and telephone),
verbal description, and plot detail. We are given two versions of the same scene, with interchangeable actors playing opposite roles, while no objective or authoritative
version of the scene is presented. The result is a wrenching of perception, a teasing perplexity about the relationship of these visualized scenes to the emotions evoked by
them. The "destiny" of created characters is prefigured
in the forms of artistic convention: the sixteenth-century

sketch is mirrored in the shape of Demon's and d'Onsky's experience.

The Parmigianino incident in *Ada* reflects the essential concern of the novel with methods of perception and creation. The author suggests that we have no evidence of how Demon made his deduction about Marina on the basis of the evidence we have read, nor are we told how the scene actually transpired (which lover was at the hotel with her, or did they both imagine such a scene without partaking in it?); but what is important is the flash of the imagined relationship between scenes and details, the artistic fitting of the past into the present through correspondence which reveals the author's design. During Marina's play and in the case of the Parmigianino sketch, it is Demon's perception and the author's conception which dominate the experience and produce flashes of compelling "reality" through private and idiosyncratic recognition and creation of an elusive meaning. The elusiveness and incompleteness of the image are stressed through the deliberate confusion of roles between the lover and his rival, so that the focus is on the act of deception and the "quotation" from Parmigianino, forming an artistic pattern.

Even the horror of madness, obsession, and death is controlled by allusive patterning, as it had been in *Bend Sinister* (most strikingly in the Shakespeare section). The death of Demon's double, Dan Veen, is placed in a Boschean setting: "Daniel Veen's life had been a mixture of the ready-made and the grotesque; but his death had shown an artistic streak because of its reflecting . . . [a] passion for the paintings . . . of Hieronymous Bosch" (p. 433). The unfolding of the Boschean nightmare takes place against the backdrop of teasingly concealed mosaics. Van puts on a "strawberry-red terry-cloth robe" (p. 434), unaware of the visual allusion which the author is setting up. The Raven-like Demon, clothed in black with a broad black monocle ribbon, reacts strangely to his son's entrance: "He gave a slight start . . . noting the coincidence of color with a persistent detail in an illumined lower left-hand corner of a certain picture reproduced in the copiously illustrated catalogue of his immediate mind" (p. 435). The red terry reappears in the story of mad Dan's final outing. Dan, who imagines himself ridden by "a devil combining the characteristics of a frog and a rodent . . . , black, pale-bellied, with a black dorsal buckler shining like a dung beetle's back and with a knife in his raised forelimb," escapes from his fiendish nurse, and, wearing "a red bath towel which trailed from his rump like a kind of caparison," crawls "into the wooded landscape" (p. 435). Demon tells Van that when Dan was found, he died "raving about that detail of the picture," "now preserved in the Vienna Academy of Art" (p. 436).

Bosch's tryptic of "The Last Judgment" (in Vienna, of course) contains on the lower left of its central panel a red-caparisoned human ridden by the black monster described above, with the added detail of what seem to be ribbon-like wings or tentacles. Demon recognizes the coincidence of the red robe and the red towel, but he himself seems to be part of the color pattern: Bosch's picture of the devil and Dan is mirrored by Demon and Van. Allusion and patterning merge in the coloring of this scene, and we get a receding level of reality where Bosch's painting is re-enacted by Dan, and in turn mirrored by Demon and Van, who are themselves manipulated by the omniscient author. Dan's death thus becomes an apotheosis into art (like Vaniada's final merging into the "blurb" of *Ada*), as he crawls "into the wooded landscape" (landscape being a formal term, and "wooded" a pun on the meaning of Bosch's name).

Demon also expresses his admiration for the incestuous meeting of art and science, the "ducal bosquet" of "that other tryptic, that tremendous garden of tongue-in-cheek delights" (p. 436), alluding to Bosch's birthplace (Hertogenbosch) and his "Garden of Earthly Delights," whose strategically placed butterflies are like *Ada's*. Demon reasserts Nabokov's emphasis on detail and texture: "I don't give a hoot for the esoteric meaning, for the myth behind the moth, . . . I am allergic to allegory and am quite sure he was just enjoying himself by cross-breeding casual fancies just for the fun of the contours and color, . . . the joy of the eye, the feel and taste of the woman-sized strawberry that you embrace *with* him" (p. 437). The chapter ends with a sudden switch back to Dan's "last sigh" about "Jeroen Anthniszoon van Äken and the *molti aspetti affascinati* of his *enigmatica arte*" (p. 438). The name is Bosch's original name, and the Italian phrases are borrowed from Mario Buscagli's *Bosch* (Firenze: Sadea Editore, 1966), p. 3. Again, Dan's dying is placed into the context of a critical "blurb" about Bosch's artistry, thereby foreshadowing the ending of *Ada*.

The title of "Garden of Earthly Delights" could be more appropriately applied to *Ada*, whose sensual delights are less ambiguous and threatened than Bosch's. *Ada* can be viewed as a tryptic of erotic pleasure similar to Bosch's: Heaven and Hell at either extreme seen as Edenic passion, and the torment and madness associated with Terra. Its main panel is a combination of the overwhelmingly joyous but occasionally shadowed landscape of passionate love; when folded, the novel has the two external panels of the Family Tree and the final "Blurb."

Both of the latter reflect the imprint of the author through the presentation of the conventions and controlled fade-out which he manipulates. (The Penguin paperback of *Ada* [Aylesbury, Bucks: Hazell Watson and Viney Ltd., 1970] has the additional panel of "Notes to *Ada*" by Nabokov masquerading as "Vivian Darkbloom" from *Lolita*.) The Bosch allusions point partly to the similarities in technique between the two artists (the huge panel teeming with self-contained yet distortedly repeated scenes, the combination of realistic and fantastic detail precisely executed, the topology of an imagined universe under the monistic control of its creator), partly to a special mode of perception.

In a sense Nabokov is asking us to read as if we were viewing a painting (unlike Bosch, he includes various styles, techniques, and allusions on the same canvas). We are being forced to read not only linearly but also circularly or spirally, with the details constantly in mind, traveling back to reflections and duplications, finding symmetrical bits of color and design amidst disparate scenes. Thus we have to reread, circle back, assemble pieces which have been placed by the author. In his notes to the Penguin edition, Nabokov tells us that most of the doctors in the book "bear names connected with rabbits" (p. 463), a technique suggesting a verbal equivalent of Bosch's half-human, half-animal figures, as well as his symmetrical spatial arrangements. Within *Ada* we are constantly asked to recollect and piece together "who, and where in this tale, in this life, had also attempted a *whispered cry*?" (p. 520); "Now who pronounced it that way? Who?" (p. 381); "the third blind character in this chronicle" (p. 468); "last call for that joke" (p. 558). The pattern is sometimes made explicit through the use of direct questions and hints, but more typically (or tryptically) we are given verbal or visual details which point to the author's design or technique. Sometimes a character or a turn in the plot acts as the visualization of methods of composition. The visual quality and imitative nature of the image of naked Marina as Eve, and dying Dan, tie in these scenes with the extremes of the Eden theme (the tree of knowledge in Van's and Ada's "first kiss," the references to Marvell's "Garden") and the elements of betrayal, agony, and suffering.

When Van visits the dying Rack after discovering that the music teacher had been having an affair with Ada, he prepares a metaphysical statement for the moribund patient: "[In death] we must face therefore the possibility of some prolonged form of disorganized consciousness and this brings me to my main point, Mr. Rack. Eternal Rack, infinite 'Rackness' may not be much but one thing is certain: the only consciousness that persists in the hereafter is the consciousness of pain. The little Rack of today is the infinite rack of tomorrow—— . . . We should imagine tiny clusters of particles still retaining Rack's personality, gathering here and there in the here-and there-after, clinging to each other, somehow, somewhere, a web of Rack's toothaches here, a bundle of Rack's nightmares there—rather like tiny groups of obscure refugees. . . . I submit that the surviving cells of aging Rackness will form such lines of torment, never, never, never reaching the covered filth hole in the panic and pain of infinite night" (pp. 314–315). The speech suggests the agony of disorganized consciousness by its very disorganization.

The emphasis on the torment of the hereafter is a subject considered in *Pnin* (where one of Pnin's "heart attacks" brings the image of his sweetheart murdered in a concentration camp), *Bend Sinister*, and *Pale Fire*. And yet, disorganized and agonizing as it may be, there is an assertion of the survival of consciousness. This speech seems to be describing a method of characterization in *Ada*: even after the fictional death of Rack, his traits will be reassigned to other characters and scenes. The authorial presence lives on in other guises, and his prose will recreate similarities and echoes of Rack. As Rack's name suggests, his character is to be a source of "bundles" of suffering and nightmares, here temporarily localized in a single character, but emerging to the surface of the narrative long after this particular embodiment dies. Prose style is the formal ordering of human consciousness in an imaginative work. Van's speech provides an insight into the manner in which *Ada* is "imagined": "The little Rack of today is the infinite rack of tomorrow" foreshadows an expansion and intensification of the theme of agony. "Disorganized consciousness" provides a central metaphor for death and madness in *Ada*. In the novel the mad believe in Terra, and the terrifying chronicle of the symptoms of Aqua's madness is characterized as "racking" (p. 21).

The theme of creativity touches the mystery of consciousness at one extreme, and deliberate patterning at the other extreme. Nabokov's characters are usually self-creating within their story, and they are also constantly in the act of being created by the author. This dual process of creation fuses the subject of imaginative self-expression with that of creative structuring. The main characters, in more or less explicit ways, are defining themselves through a narrative they are composing and acting out. Nabokov's frequent reversions to dramatic techniques and stage directions underline the suggestion that his characters are simultaneously shaping an illusory reality and yet retaining an awareness of the workings of artifice.[5] Like actors, these characters manifest both an

[5] For an excellent treatment of the artificiality of Nabokov's

absorption in their roles and a detachment from their assumed personalities. They view their personalities as artistic façades built of carefully assembled patterns. Most of Nabokov's novels create the impression that one or more characters are authors of their own stories and yet actors within the larger scheme of the omniscient creator.

4

Van is the main character, narrator, and author—the omniscient author appears perhaps as the English tourist in Kim's photograph of the "apotheosis of Ardis," which features the "entire staff" (pp. 406–407). The tourist is a "terribly tweedy gentleman with sightseeing trappings" who came to see "Bryant's Castle" (i.e., Chateaubriand) but lost his way. Ada swears that he "was, and has always remained, a complete stranger" (p. 408) (like the author who is not known to his characters at the end of *Sebastian Knight*). This, like the moth-catching Englishman of "Spring in Fialta,"[6] may be the author's assertion of his distance from his work. He is part of the cast, but merely as a chance visitor, uninvolved in the passion and torture of the characters, "sightseeing" the patterns and details which form the narrative. Originally seeking the romantic despair of Chateaubriand's imaginative castle of incestuous love—both Van and Ada read Chateaubriand's work[7] —he has wandered into another version of that theme, a

---

dramas, see Simon Karlinsky, "Illusion, Reality and Parody in Nabokov's Plays," in the Dembo anthology, pp. 183–195.

[6] See B. H. Monter, " 'Spring in Fialta': The Choice That Mimics Chance," in the *Tri-Quarterly* anthology, pp. 128–136.

[7] As noted in Alter's illuminating essay on *Ada* (*Tri-Quarterly* anthology, pp. 48–49), and Alfred Appel's "*Ada* Described," pp. 175–179.

manor which, we are assured, is "quite worth inspecting
too."

Sight is a major element of memory and recollection
in *Ada,* just as it had been in *Pale Fire.* Shade's "stillicide"
and his vision of the fountain are duplicated and expanded
in Van's imaginative "sightseeing" of novelistic conventions, refracted images of passionate love, and landscapes
of madness and death. Kinbote the Peeping Tom is played
by Kim, whose pornographic album Ada calls "crippled
art" (p. 406), and whose artistic crudeness is fittingly
(if brutally) punished by his being blinded (a blinding
which can be pieced together on pages 441 and 446 by the
careful rereader).

There are fleeting images of the author throughout the
book, as in the list of the Circus Company in which Van
performs. Among the defectors to the West is "a make-
up man (no doubt a multiple agent)" (p. 181), again emphasizing the freedom and versatility of the "agent"
who may be assumed to be in the cast, but whose imaginative ("make-up") facility allows escape. (*Lolita's* "Rita"
appears in the silver slippers of the ballerina from *Sebastian Knight* as the dancer married to the "make-up
fellow" [p. 185].) Another detached observer-creator figure, this time a painter, is glimpsed by Van and Ada on
the day when Demon discovers their affair and they have
to part: "An aproned man stood there setting up an
easel and cocking his head in search of the right angle"
(p. 439). Critics who are puzzled by the moral tone taken
by Demon and accepted by his children in this amoral
chronicle[8] might recall *Lolita's* "palliative of articulate

[8] See M. Dickstein, "Nabokov's Folly," *New Republic,* June 28,
1969, p. 28. Similar questions about Nabokov's fiction having
"soul," or ultimate seriousness, are raised by Anthony Burgess'
"Poet and Pedant," *Spectator,* March 24, 1967, p. 337, and by
William H. Gass' "Mirror, Mirror" in *Fiction and the Figures of
Life* (New York: Knopf 1970), pp. 110–119.

art. . . . 'The moral sense in mortals is the duty / We have to pay on mortal sense of beauty' " (p. 258). The morality of Nabokov's art is dictated by emotional criteria distanced through the author's irony. The chapter which culminates in Demon's discovery of the affair begins with an assertion of omniscience: "They took a great many precautions—all absolutely useless, for nothing can change the end (written and filed away) of the present chapter" (p. 432). This suggests the enslavement of the characters to the author's whims, and places the "moral" decision within the framework of the artistically predetermined formal pattern.

Both chapters dealing with Demon's discovery are full of painterly effects. Like the Parmigianino sketch, the use of the Bosch tryptic is an example of time artistically perceived: the painted and the novelistic image are conflated and become temporally simultaneous through the artistic perception. Time can be measured only through the vividness of images and metaphors, not in terms of objective chronology, and the arrangement of images through allusion or repetition renders time ancillary to art. The interweaving of Dan's death with Van's and Ada's parting provides a framework of suffering within artistic control.

In Chapter 11 we see Demon in a "gray" gown on a grey couch (in Chapter 10 he was "all in black"), in visual terms" as if all color were drained from the mind" (p. 439). Seen through Demon's grey "fatigue," Van and Ada's affair is drained of its festive colors of brightness, joy, and unique pleasure; it becomes harmful, conventional, judged by clichés. The "banal" (p. 439), "neutral" (p. 442) nature of the scene is observed by the narrator and the characters. Demon insists on "normal" relationships, "the tritest terms," and ends with a paternal curse and sobs. The artificiality of the scene is emphasized by theatrical terminology, the authorial insertion of a lengthy flashback of Black Miller and flashforward of blackmailers (pp. 440–441).

Demon's request sounds like a parody of hackneyed fictional renunciations: "If you love her, you wish her to be happy, and she will not be as happy as she could be once you gave her up" (p. 444). Van's farewell letter to Ada recognizes a necessity to yield, "You see, girl, how it is and must be," but, in a seeming *non sequitur*, continues, as if to explain his decision: "In the last window we shared we both saw a man painting [us?] but your second-floor level of vision probably prevented your seeing that he wore what looked like a butcher's apron, badly smeared" (p. 445). (Van and Demon are on the third floor, Ada on the second floor beneath them, and the painter across the lane is opposite the third floor.) Van's letter reflects back to the artist composing the scene which has just taken place. Van and Ada "share the last window" or panel because they are elements in a single artistic vision, even when they are placed on receding planes of perception. The artist faces Van directly, perhaps because Van is a primary character and also an artist figure, but Ada appears at a different angle in the scene: she is an aspect of Van's consciousness, in some ways she is a secondary character.

The sequence of "how it must be" and the painter ties together the hint of the inevitable unfolding of action with the artist who is composing the scene. Van's "moral sense" (to return to the terms of the *Lolita* quotation) is no more than the yielding to the preordained narrative, to the author's artistic sense of proportion, movement, perspective. Van's decision to obey Demon is deliberately arbitrary and unexplained, as if to point to the unarguable hand of the omniscient author who rules the characters. The painter has plotted the entire picture, and his characters glimpse him through the windowpane, where he appears simultaneously as a reflected character in the scene as well as its creator. The detail of the "butcher's apron, badly smeared" suggests that Van perhaps attributes a degree of sadism or brutality to the author who so capriciously separates his lovers, but it may be that the apron is smeared with the pigment of the scene we are observing. (There might be a pun on the painter Boucher.) In either case, the artist remains apart, manipulating the lives and emotions of his characters according to aesthetic considerations ("sense of beauty"), wrenching lives and canvases from a distance.

In Nabokov the distinction between the fictional artist figures such as Humbert, Van, Shade, and the intrusions of the author into the narrative—either as a voice or as a visualized character—is emphasized. These two aspects of the artist are usually quite separate in Nabokov's work, but function as complementary aspects of a total portrait of the artist. While the fictional artists are allowed to express their perversions, sentiments, and anxieties, the omniscient author appears calm, in control, superior, often mocking. The result of this juxtaposition is a blend of subjective and objective attitudes toward the artistic process and personality. The subjective reaction allows the emotional "reality" of death, suffering, and ecstasy, while the objective overview places the emotion in a stylistic perspective, insisting that these feelings are a "play on words," "a question of technique." The author, by means of his craftsmanship, divests himself of the agony of his fictional artist-characters. Often the artist-characters attempt to control and record their emotions through the creation of a work of art: thus we have a receding regression of portraits of creativity. The artist-character is often viewed through a distance imparted by some flaw or obsession such as Humbert's perversion, V.'s ordinariness, Van's haughtiness and libertinism, or self-parodies within the work.

In many of Nabokov's works we see artist figures who are mad, perverted, obsessed, flawed. And yet their work is often of surpassing beauty, as if to demonstrate the process of reverse mirroring whereby the reflection of the exterior world can produce an imaginative vision of compelling "reality" through the consciousness of ludicrous characters. But Nabokov usually insists on pointing out (through a change of voice, or a shifting to the author toward the end of the work) that these ludicrous or flawed artist-characters are distorted puppet-images of the omniscient author. The flawed artist can contemplate his experience through the mirror of his consciousness and produce a vision of beauty. Since art is a kind of mirror-reversal, opposing qualities such as cruelty and suffering are often transformed into, or at least are made to suggest, tenderness and ecstasy.

The intrusion of the author into the narrative can also take the form of patterning: the recurring puddle, imprint, "sanglot" injected into the work often without the fictional artist's awareness. Through these patterns we glimpse not the actual figure or voice of the author but the shape of his artistry on the surface texture of his work. This kind of artistic self-portrait makes for a multiple perspective where the artist is just another figure on the mirrored plane of his art. But both the actual appearances of the author (as one of the hunters in Quilty's play, as the conjurer and the ultimate, unknown presence in *Sebastian Knight*, as the Russian writer in *Pnin* and at the end of *Pale Fire*, and the moth-catcher in *Bend Sinister*) and his patterned footprints remain emotionally detached, spatial, compositional elements. These authorial images and patterns rarely touch on the author's moral or emotional preferences; they stress his magical powers, his omniscience, his calm playfulness, his intricate sense of form. The author's portrait is never a confession or a psychological revelation; it is a gleeful image of the chess-master, butterfly-hunter revealing his hand or his net, but not his motives or anxieties. Sometimes Nabokov contrasts the gentle and pathetic fictional character with the egocentric author figure (*Pnin*), sometimes the pity of the author "saves" an admirable character from anguish (Krug's madness in *Bend Sinister*).

Most of Nabokov's novels are concerned with the artist in the act of writing. Since the "real" subjects and objects which he is writing about are already selected, described, and fitted into a fictional pattern in the act of choosing them, even these "realities" are seen as through a mirror or a prism. The artist, the nature of his prose style, and even the work we are reading are often viewed through the distancing of a mirror, so that we have frames, or receding fictional planes. An effect of mirroring is sometimes achieved by representing different aspects of the artist in different characters (Mlle. Larivière, Kim, Ada, Van), parodies of possible descriptions of the prose style of the work (in *Lolita, Sebastian Knight, Ada*), or interior reflections distortedly multiplying the plot and details which occur in most of Nabokov's novels. The world being described, the artist figure, and the work of art are seen as elements and products of the creative imagination. *Pale Fire* explores the relationship of these elements to each other and to the problem of death. The act of creation, the purpose of art seen by Renaissance and neo-classical literature as "holding a mirror up to nature," in Nabokov's work becomes not simply holding a mirror up to the self, but holding a mirror up to the mirror of the self seen in the process of creation. The multiplicity of the artist figure, seen in the imaginative act of creation, is the major subject of Nabokov's works.

The artist figures are refractions of the author; but curiously, when the author appears he suggests a solidity and a "reality" amidst his fictional creations. The author as artificer is "real" because he is in full control of his figments, and he frequently breaks the fictional illusion with a confident statement of the solidity of his own existence. Through the consciousness of his "otherness" from his fiction, the author often appears as the manipulator not only of his artist figures, but also of various representations of himself within and outside his fiction.

The author's voice frequently intrudes to suggest that his recurrent themes such as hopeless love, perversion, death, and obsession are in turn metaphoric of various aspects of artistic creation. He emphasizes the passionate pursuit of the private obsession which turns into a tender love for a particular subject (*Lolita*), the artist's ability both to annihilate and recreate himself through his art (*Pale Fire, Sebastian Knight*), the imagination debased by vulgar or trite modes of perception (*Laughter in the Dark, King, Queen and Knave*, and commercial-artist figures such as Quilty, Axel, Goodman). The exploration of these themes asserts the supremacy of the subjectively determined perception. Nabokov unabashedly manipulates his characters to give the reader glimpses of the artistic rules by which they perform.[9] The rules comprise various patterns in which hopeless love, death, perversion, and obsession are related to the artist's vision of "tenderness, kindness, ecstasy" (*Lolita*, p. 286).

As this manipulative process implies, most of Nabokov's characters are either shifting masks of the author or fleeting dramatizations of temporal-spatial relationships. "Consistency of characterization" is not a rule by which we can measure Nabokov's figments. Even when the main

[9] See note 12, Chapter IV.

characters of his novels possess a fairly stable identity (as in *Lolita*), we are usually aware of the work as an "artifice" and of its main character as actor and artificer. The world of the novels hovers above, and only distortedly and incidentally reflects empirical reality.[10]

In order to parody outworn conventions and banal fictional rules, Nabokov often weaves a "sham" pattern into his works: clues to mislead the imperceptive, traditional themes which feign to sustain the narrative, apparently easy solutions to mysteries. But the genuine emphasis is on the details and involutions of the style and the conception; the parody often reinforces the originality of tone. As V. writes of one of his fictional doubles, Sebastian Knight: He "was ever hunting out the things which had once been fresh and bright but which were now worn to a thread, dead things among living ones; dead things shamming life, painted and repainted, continuing to be accepted by lazy minds serenely unaware of the fraud. . . . He did not mind in the least 'penny dreadfuls' because he wasn't concerned with ordinary morals; what annoyed him invariably was the second rate, not the third or n-th rate, because here, at the readable stage, the shamming began, and this was, in an *artistic* sense, immoral" (pp. 91–92). Machine-made, unreflecting intelligence characterizes many of Nabokov's villains, like Gradus of *Pale Fire* who is finally no more than an unpleasant figment of the imagination, a tool for providing an ending. For Nabokov, what is immoral is to pander to the reader's ready-made assumptions about literature and reality, to bring about no artistic revelation in the reader's consciousness, to make

[10] At the end of Nabokov's novel *The Gift*, the hero recapitulates the abstract plot of the novel whose main character he has been, and remarks: "Now isn't that the plot for a remarkable novel? What a theme! But it must be built up, curtained, surrounded by dense life" (pp. 375–376).

no impression of delight or wonder through the perception of design.

Beyond the sham and parodic patterns is another, more elusive design. This subliminal design follows the essential quest for the meaning of the involutions of life; a quest conducted through an exploration of the coincidences created by conscious artistry. When the disparate clues do not fit into a patterned design, the effect is of a "quest" "grading into delirium," a feeling which Pnin experiences during his heart attacks (p. 24), Humbert during his search for guilty Quilty. It seems to me a mistaken simplification to call the process and the result of Nabokov's quest an "escape into aesthetics," as Stegner does, even if one regards the formula as honorific. Nabokov does not offer an aesthetic of evasion or retreat, or willful denial of physical reality. He insists, rather, on the freedom to present his own version of this reality; a version of brilliantly and boldly inventive iridescence which mirrors the pain and rapture of perception. Nabokov persistently emphasizes that imaginative reality is twofold: it may mirror the materials of the physical world, but its essence lies in transforming these materials into the special shape and "coloration" of the writer's fantasy. *Sebastian Knight* describes the process of the quest for individual truth as a "dream" which uses the "pattern of reality for the weaving of its own fancies" (p. 137).

Nabokov, like his fictional reflection, Sebastian, searches for the methods of "fate" (or McFate, as he is called in *Lolita*) in the lives which he creates. "Fate" in his fiction is a combination of stylistic technique, detailed patterning, and imaginative leaps. The composite of this combination constitutes the "web of sense" Shade discovers through his poetry (p. 63). This "web of sense" is the unique logic and lucidity of the laws governing

Nabokov's individual works; "Fate" is manifested in patterns unfolding through the vision of the artist. Methods of fate converge in art; the inscrutable "nonsense" of life is given direction and a pattern of subjective "sense." Art is the glass which distortedly duplicates or doubles the flow of life.[11] In addition to the doubling of characters (Hermann and his false double, Sebastian and V., Humbert-Quilty, Pnin-Tvynn, the sibling lovers of *Ada, etc.*), there is a frequent distorted doubling of action (narrative events seen as alternate fictional possibilities or a "forking" when a character "dies" but continues to exist).

Sebastian Knight abounds in reference to puddles which seem to be metaphoric of the beautiful interior reflections provided by Sebastian's own novels within the novel. The puddles connect the reality of Sebastian's fiction with that of his half-brother's fiction and with the reality of the artist behind the entire action. In *Pnin* after the whole fictional cast is temporarily asleep, the narrator remarks that "It was a pity nobody saw the display in the empty street, where the auroral breeze wrinkled a large luminous puddle, making of the telephone wires reflected in it illegible lines of black zigzags" (p. 110). In this image the author calls attention to the beauty of what he is creating for us, the display which shines through the sleeping characters. The "illegible lines of black zigzags," unnoticed in the rush of everyday life, are controlled and made legible by the perception beneath the puddle. Through the puddle the reader glimpses the translucence of the fictional world; a sudden opening reveals the author's undisguised imprint. The puddles in *Bend Sinister* lead from the perception of the fictional character Krug

[11] An especially suggestive article on the double and mirror theme, though it does not deal with Nabokov specifically, is O. Maslenikov's "Russian Symbolists: The Mirror Theme and Allied Motifs," *The Russian Review* (January, 1957), pp. 42–52.

to the vision of his creator, who sees a "special puddle" in the final paragraph and compares it to the "imprint we leave in the intimate texture of space" (p. 222).

As Nabokov explains in a special edition of *Bend Sinister*, the puddle is "a rent in [Krug's] world leading to another world of tenderness, brightness, beauty,"[12] the world of artistic creation as defined in his Afterword to *Lolita*. Thus the puddle, and its variants such as the mirror and the windowpane, is an aperture through which we see not only the controlling hand of the artist, but also the values connected with Nabokov's conception of art. The pattern which emanates from these rents in the surface of the fictional landscape chronicles a quest which renders illegible lines into an intense experience of "tenderness, brightness, beauty." In each novel the pattern varies and the experience fluctuates between intense emotional involvement, intellectual pleasure, and "that golden and monstrous peace" produced by the precise word or glowing phrase which lovers of language can only term passion.

[12] *Bend Sinister* (New York: *Time Reading Program* Special Edition, 1964), Foreword, p. xv.